Reach Up For The Sunrise

A Duran Duran Biography

Jen Selinsky

This book is dedicated to my friend, Marco, who is kind enough to believe in my work.

Reach Up For The Sunrise

A Duran Duran Biography

Jen Selinsky

WP
WYMER
PUBLISHING
Bedford, England

First published in Great Britain in 2021
by Wymer Publishing
www.wymerpublishing.co.uk
Tel: 01234 326691
Wymer Publishing is a trading name of Wymer (UK) Ltd

Copyright © 2021 Wymer Publishing.
Copyright © 2006, 2016 by Jen Selinsky

ISBN: 978-1-912782-72-7
(also available in eBook)

Edited by Stephen Francis

The Author hereby asserts his rights to be identified
as the author of this work in accordance with sections
77 to 78 of the Copyright, Designs & Patents Act 1988.

All rights reserved. No part of this publication may be
reproduced or transmitted in any form or by any means,
electronic or mechanical, including photocopying, or any
information storage and retrieval system, without written
permission from the publisher.

This publication is sold subject to the condition that it shall not,
by way of trade or otherwise, be lent, re-sold, hired out or
otherwise circulated without the publishers prior consent in any
form of binding or cover other than that in which it is published
and without a similar condition including this condition
being imposed on the subsequent purchaser.

Every effort has been made to trace the copyright holders of the
photographs in this book but some were unreachable. We would
be grateful if the photographers concerned would contact us.

Typeset by Andy Bishop / 1016 Sarpsborg
Printed by CMP, Dorset, England.

A catalogue record for this book is available from the British Library.

Cover design: Andy Bishop / 1016 Sarpsborg
Front cover image © Fraser Gray / Alamy Stock Photo
Back cover image © Yui Mok, PA Images / Alamy Stock Photo

CONTENTS

Preface	7
Chapter 1: In The Beginning	13
Chapter 2: The Man in the Pink Leopard Skin Trousers	29
Chapter 3: Heyday	35
Chapter 4: Times in the Life of Simon Le Bon	63
Chapter 5: The Breakup	69
Chapter 6: Moving Along	77
Chapter 7: Dreaming of a Big Thing	87
Chapter 8: Knock, Knock, Remember Us?	99
Chapter 9: Covering Others	109
Chapter 10: Another Taylor Takes Leave	117
Chapter 11: And Then There Were Three	125
Chapter 12: The Strongest Comeback!	131
Chapter 13: Saying Goodbye for a Second Time	151
Chapter 14: Going Back to Their Roots	161
Chapter 15: What Happens Tomorrow?	179
Afterword	183
Discography	184
References	187
About The Author	192

PREFACE

Welcome Duranies from all around the world. I know many of you have been fans of Duran Duran for years and have collected as many items by, and about, them as you possibly could. Allow me to add something new to your collection. I hope you will get enjoyment and insight from what you are about to read.

You've looked for something new, and now you will find that your patience has paid off. This, my friends, is a book about Duran Duran's life and career from their beginnings to the present day. The following work contains information which many of you may have known for years, although, I am hoping that some of it will be new to you.

Reach up for the Sunrise explores both the highlights and low points that the members of Duran Duran have experienced, both as a band and as individuals. Through this work, one can witness the wonder of their lives and music unfold and be explored. Since there is a lot of ground to cover, let us enter into the fascinating world of Duran Duran.

I know that some of you may be hesitant to embark upon this journey. You may be thinking, *Why is this woman writing a book about Duran Duran, and who exactly is she, anyway?* Well, I can give you so many answers to the question, especially since I became a fan of the band in 2000. But I will only stick to the main points I want to address.

The band has given me inspiration for so many things, and their music always seems to do the trick when I feel my spirit needs uplifting. They have also helped me through the lengthy papers that I had to write for some of my courses in college. One of my professors even let me do my senior project on them, a paper evaluation on three videos of Duran Duran! I evaluated "Save a Prayer," "Night Boat," and "Hungry Like the Wolf." Just the fact that I was allowed to write something about my favourite subject was enough to make me enthusiastic for the rest of the semester.

That was a minor work made available to the "public," which was comprised of my professor and classmates. Even though I faltered a little during the presentation, my professor was ultimately impressed with my overall work, and I received a good grade. Others who have later read the paper enjoyed it, even those who are not necessarily fans of Duran Duran. This raised my level of confidence and gave me enough courage to embark upon this challenging project.

I purchased my first Duran Duran album in 1994, a copy of *Decade*, on cassette. That is when I gained a slight interest in the band. I started to learn more songs than "Rio," "Hungry Like the Wolf," and the two most popular singles from *The Wedding Album*. I listened to them on and off for the next six years, until Duran Duran became my favourite band in May 2000.

The first time I got to see them in concert was on August 13, 2000 at the I.C. Light Amphitheatre in Pittsburgh, and it was one of the greatest nights of my life. After that, it was the Trib Total Media Amphitheatre, located in Station Square, until it finally closed down. I finally got to witness what all the excitement was about; it was truly a wonderful experience. Right then and there, I was mesmerised.

I knew immediately that I would be forever be changed by this group and would always be enamoured by all things Duran Duran. I held on to my fascination, and I will continue to do so because, every day, I find myself more and more drawn to their music and talent.

Concerts were always wonderful events, and people would be surprised not only by the fact that I am a writer but that I am also a Duranie. My age and general knowledge of the band seemed to have an interesting effect on others as well. I remember people being fascinated at how much initial information I could give them before the band came out on stage.

I would rattle off names, birthdates, and most anything else that involved the band in any way. Most other fans seemed to like the fact that I knew as much as I did.

Some of the most interesting experiences I've had regarding the band include getting curious stares from my fellow concert goers. People would take a close look at me and say, "*You're* a fan of Duran Duran?"

I would nod my head and tell them how long I have been interested in the band.

They would then ask, "Just how *old* are you, anyway?"

When I told them that I was in my mid-twenties, they would find themselves a little surprised because many people think I look younger than my actual age. They wondered just how someone "your age could have become interested in the band."

When I saw Duran Duran perform in Louisville, Kentucky in March 2005, one of the gentlemen behind me asked what I was doing

Preface

when the song "The Wild Boys" was No.1 on the charts. I simply replied with something like, "I don't know, I was probably out in the backyard playing or something. I was only five or six."

Of course, at that age, I had only seen two of their videos on MTV, and I remember being a little scared of "Hungry Like the Wolf" and "Rio" when I was about four because I did not understand the actual content and sexual connotations of the songs.

One of my favourite things from the 2005 concerts was the Duran Duran "anime film," which was backed by the song "Careless Memories." That actually served as the original cover for my book.

I know many of you are long-time fans who have followed the band ever since their inception, and that is one of the reasons why I find it easy to admire you. I'll go ahead and admit, right now, that I did not start becoming what some would call a "real" fan of Duran Duran until right before the release of their tenth studio album, *Pop Trash*, a work, which likely, was not known by those who are not Duranies.

To make a long story short, a few months before I truly discovered their music, I experienced a strong desire to hear the song "Ordinary World." I had the song stuck in my head on the drive back from one of my college classes. That was the beginning of my new fascination. I dug out my cassette tape copy of *Decade* and the other three albums which I had purchased. I decided that I wanted to hear more of their music, so I bought the rest of their albums as soon as I could get my fingers on them.

I have listened to the band a lot during these last sixteen years, and so many good things have come from their music. That is the short version because the rest of the explanation would probably constitute roughly enough information for an autobiography.

First of all, to my knowledge, this is one of the few books that have been written about the band in a while, not including Andy Taylor's and John Taylor's autobiographies, with the exception of Steve Malins' biographies, *Notorious*, then later, *Wild Boys* and *Duran Duran: Unseen* by Paul Edmond. And while this one isn't chalked full of dozens of photographs of the band, those which are included will be sure to delight my fellow Duranies.

Here and there, a few books on Duran Duran have been published, but they mostly provide the music and lyrics for some albums and songs, such as the music book accompanying *The Wedding Album*, which contains music for piano, vocal, and guitar. Of course, when I saw it, (like most avid collectors) I knew I had to go ahead and buy it, even though I don't know how to play either guitar or piano.

Since some of you may not have read any books on the band for a while, it probably is safe to assume that many of you are no longer fourteen or fifteen years old, so we can rely more on the written word rather than the handsome visuals which are etched in our minds.

This book spans their full career, starting from their beginning in 1978, (which was also my beginning) through to early 2021.

I feel that Duran Duran has done a phenomenal job of sustaining their career during the recent years and keeping their name in the media. Their music has captivated people for over four decades, and the recent success of their latest album has caught the attention of a younger audience. They are one of the surviving bands from the 1980s which has been able to receive almost as much success with the audiences of today as they did back in what was commonly referred to as their "heyday."

This is one of the reasons why I have embarked on this arduous task, so that I can at least temporarily remedy the situation. To be honest, until very recently, I was tired of going into bookstores and asking for materials on Duran Duran and having the clerks scoff and/or show me total indifference. They seemed surprised there was still a demand for information about the band. I was also sick and tired of seeing other bands, especially contemporary artists and others who were not as well-known as Duran Duran, having books about them available for the general public.

When I went to bookstores with my friends, I would turn to them and say, "This really bothers me, how there are no more books on Duran Duran. If this keeps up, I am going to have to write one myself to try and fill the void on the shelves." Of course, some people might have thought I was joking, but most of my friends knew just how serious I am about this band, so many of them probably didn't put it past me.

All this recent excitement has helped me get inspired to start on this fun and exciting project. Just like the boys of Duran Duran had dreams of making the world know their music and talent, I have my own dream of giving back to the band, and their fans, what they have given to me during the greatest years of my life. I figured that I had to put an end to the shortage of Duran Duran books on the shelves in the bookstores, and you, the other fans, deserve it, especially those who have been so loyal to everything Duran over the years.

This is your time to have your appreciation looked upon and taken seriously. Many of the other books written about Duran Duran were created by journalists and other professional writers who had little interest in the band and only wanted to produce a pop culture book without regards to any particular group.

This book was written by a genuine fan, who has shown her devotion to the band, no matter the ups and downs they have gone through. Through my ideas and presentation of the information, I will tell the story of Duran Duran from a fan's point of view. Now, you will be able to read all about the band from the perspective of someone who admires them just as much as you do.

I also want to take a moment to express my gratitude to the band for giving me the inspiration to improve my life. It was because of their music that I have been able to discover another aspect that is important to me, my health. Most every day, I worked out to their music and lost weight as a result. Since then, I have been inspired to live a healthier lifestyle and enjoy the time that I spend exercising to their music.

I have also been inspired to create many works of art, both related and unrelated to the band. Duran Duran has stimulated both my mind and my body, two very important things, which I took for granted before.

As both a band and individuals, Duran Duran has overcome many obstacles, and since their reunion in 2003 and through the release of *Paper Gods*, they have been selling out shows faster than people can even say their name.

The turn of events is nothing short of phenomenal, and I'm sure that I'm not the only one who wishes to offer the band their congratulations.

Many fans, even those younger than myself, find that they cannot resist the natural charm that radiated from the band. It is the very same charm that they exhibited thirty years ago when they were selling out shows and serenading their most devoted of fans.

I would also say that it is time to give credit where credit is due, don't you think? Duran Duran is truly great and will go down in history as a talented and charismatic group who set the standards for video music in the eighties through present day.

I have done my best to make sure all the information I provided is accurate, and I avoided uses of direct quotations. I have also borrowed some information from books, newspaper and magazine articles, and some information that I found on the Internet. I made sure that I cited the author(s) and/or publishing companies, or sites at the end of the book in the references section.

Since some of the more current material, I am very excited to include it, especially for those fans who've renewed their interest in the band since 1985. Many of you may be wondering what happened to the band during the most recent years.

So sit back, relax, and feel free to pull out any old records that you happen to have handy. Dust them off and play them because I am going to take you on a long, fun, and factual journey. Through my own insight and research taken from other sources relating to the band; I am going to explain to you the phenomenon which is Duran Duran.

Several years have passed since I wrote the first edition of *Reach Up for the Sunrise*. While I made further revisions between 2005 and 2006, the original publication date, I did not make the decision to update the book until very recently. Truth be told, I stopped listening to Duran Duran, for the most part, because my tastes in music have changed.

My husband introduced me to music from the sixties and seventies, and I became a great fan of classic rock. Genesis, Badfinger, The Beatles, Deep Purple, and Pink Floyd are now among some of my new favourites. Duran Duran was not very high on my list of musical priorities anymore.

All that changed, however, when I purchased a copy of *All You Need Is Now* in March 2011. Since then, I have rekindled my interest in Duran Duran, and I wanted another chance to present you, the reader, with new information about the band since my book's first publication in 2006.

Enjoy.

CHAPTER 1

In the Beginning

It was the end of the punk rock era, and disco began to see its last days. The world just came down off its rock 'n' roll high from the fifties, sixties and early seventies. Rock gave way to new forms of music during the mid-seventies. While the early style of rock 'n' roll became immortalised, some people had grown tired of listening to the same type of music for years at a time. Both listeners and musicians wanted something new to reflect the changing world all around them.

The face of music was changing, and experimentation with sound was the basis for this for many groups. Youth who were interested in music went along with these changing times as best as they could by providing what they thought was the most unique thing that others have heard. Many of them grew tired of the music that was popular in the past and welcomed the change with open ears. Experimentation was what everything was about, and these young people everywhere were starting to discover the kinds of things that they liked when it came to music.

The changes in sound from the mid to the late 1970s became inherent in the work of some of the performers from that time. Having listened to the work of popular groups, such as The Beatles, Pink Floyd, Led Zeppelin, and The Doors, new musicians gathered ideas of their own.

The glam rock movement that became popular in the seventies, was spearheaded by performers such as David Bowie, who performed briefly as Ziggy Stardust. The growth of his fan base and popularity had a lot to do with the new sound. Glam rock became mainstream in England and was catching on in some of the most popular clubs and pubs in the country. People who were intrigued by this style of music became inspired to make some of their own.

Reach Up For The Sunrise

By 1978, with Glam rock then just a memory, the subsequent Punk explosion having morphed into New Wave, it was the year when the whole thing started for Duran Duran, and it was all thanks to John Taylor. He was responsible for gathering many of the ideas in his head and portraying them to the world.

Needless to say, John was very influenced by the popular music that was played during his early teenage years, and experimentation had practically become his middle name. He had great visions in his head, and he thought these visions were going to take him very far. Although John had a good level of confidence, little did he know just how much his influence on a new band would mean to the world.

Nigel John Taylor IV was born on June 20, 1960, in the Sorrento Maternity Hospital in Moseley, Birmingham (closed in 1993), and ended up his parents' only child. His mother, Jean, was a children's schoolteacher, and his father, Jack, was a car components worker, one of the few white-collar jobs in the industry. He had also fought in the war. Jack had long since retired before John's earliest days of fame.

John had a happy childhood and has fond memories of his growing up. He was exceptionally close to his mother, and they got along very well. Ironically enough, the place where John grew up was called Hollywood, a village just south of Birmingham. Of course, as funny as that sounds, no one really thought much of it at the time because the irony had yet to strike.

As many of you may already know, John was a very imaginative child and has always had a great interest in art. He was highly encouraged by his parents to pursue this activity. John was well-behaved in school, but his teachers didn't take long to notice that he was very talkative during class. He attended Our Lady of the Wayside Junior School and then Redditch Grammar School. While he excelled in his art, reading, and writing classes, John didn't do as well in mathematics and physical education.

John always had an inquisitive mind, and his love for knowledge existed outside of the classroom. He had a cosy and comfortable childhood, as he loved his home life and relished the attention of being an only child. Jack was proud of the fact that John was as interested in knowledge as he was, and the two of them would bond by Jack quizzing John about various things, including rivers and the countries of their sources.

John has indicated that his dislike for his birth name, Nigel, started when he was in grammar school. The other kids had made fun of his moniker. Nigel, after all, was represented as a geeky name in pop culture references. Since John didn't like the name he dropped it during his mid-teens and adopted his middle name as his first name. Looking back on things nowadays, however, John stated that he would have stuck with his original name because of the high number of performers named John in the music business.

During his early teens, he also found that he had an affinity for cars, and he sat in his classroom dreaming of automobile models that he would like to own instead of focusing on his class work, especially during his mathematics courses.

John was also a stylish chap who was not afraid to show others what he liked to wear. During a *Billboard Style Influence* video, released in 2015, John revealed that one of his greatest fashion influences was Frank Sinatra. Even though John had a little difficulty coming up with framing his sentence, he said that he liked Sinatra's style because Sinatra was smooth, but edgy.

John took music classes during his high school years, and since he now plays bass guitar, one can always guess what instrument he wanted to focus on in band class, guitar. Since he was stuck within the constraints of a traditional school, John was told by one of his music teachers that guitar wasn't the kind of instrument he could play in a school band because it was neither serious nor traditional enough to match the school's reputation. But John didn't care about tradition because he had his heart set on playing the guitar.

Sometime later, he tried to reach a compromise and suggested that he could play the saxophone instead. That choice was also denied, so the frustrated student decided that he was going to teach himself how to play the instrument of his choice outside of school, and he did. Later, however, he admitted to having regretted that he never took any of the piano lessons that the school had offered him.

One of the bands which John admired the most in his teens was Aerosmith, who he had seen in concert many times. He was especially fond of Joe Perry's work, and he wanted to play the guitar just like him. John remembered wanting to jump onto the stage, grabbing the guitar right out of Joe's hands, and start playing it himself! While John was studying art at Birmingham University, he toyed with the idea of creating a band of his own.

During that time, John had played in various bands, such as Dada and Shock Treatment. He had incorporated his ideas into a lot of his schoolwork. With red, black, and white pens, he began making various posters with letters scrawled all over them. This new fascination consumed him and was in his head night and day. The dream began to take over most of his eighteen-year-old life.

It seemed like John didn't want to do much else, and if he wanted his dream to come true, he knew that he had to act on his newfound interest nearly every waking moment of the day. For his final project in his art class, John handed in a demo tape of his recorded work, and nothing else.

Needless to say, his teacher was disappointed, but John passed the course, anyway. John didn't care however, because he knew what he wanted to do, set the world on fire, and he was going to let everyone know of his potential.

Time and circumstance were on his side all along, but it took him a while to realise it. It so happened that he had a very good friend whom he had known most of his life, Nicholas Bates. Nick has since changed his last name to Rhodes for what he calls "aesthetic reasons."

Nick also had some interesting sources in mind when he was searching for a last name. Firstly, he thought of the Greek island; next was the Fender Rhodes piano. Nick also thought that he would like to have the same name of The Clash's manager, Bernie Rhodes. With three different sources of inspiration, Nick thought that he couldn't go wrong and changed his name to Rhodes.

Nick and John befriended each other around the time John was ten years old, and they spent a lot of their youth together, growing even closer in their friendship. John and Nick grew up on the same Birmingham street and spent much of their childhood together. John knew that Nick would definitely be interested in his ideas, so it didn't take him long to call on his friend.

Nicholas James Bates was born nearly two years later on June 8, 1962; he was also the only child of Sylvia and Roger Bates. Sylvia was a contented housewife and mother, and Roger was an engineer. Nick also liked the idea of fame at a young age, so he took John up on his offer and joined the band when he was only sixteen years old. He was glad that he was helping his friend while gaining worldly experience at the same time.

It was not much of a secret that the young Mr. Bates was not a big fan of school. Once during an interview, he was asked to describe his

In The Beginning

childhood. Aside from Nick mentioning that his first memory was of him mixing up stones with his mother's potatoes, when he was about two, he described his kindergarten experience as being nothing short of harrowing.

In his depiction, the teacher was compared to a mean and ugly dragon, who was trying to teach the rest of the "idiots" (as he called his classmates) and him how to read. And as Nick grew up, until he reached the age of sixteen, he reflected the same dislike for school, if not much greater than when he first started. It's not that Nick was particularly a bad student, but he felt that most of his so-called "education" was a waste of time.

Nick has always been a sensitive and compassionate person, and that was revealed early in his life. He had a great understanding of people as a result of his extended compassion. His kind and gentle nature proved he had a great love for many things, especially animals. Cats were his favourite. He once owned a black tomcat named Sebastian, who was said to have lived a long and happy life.

Nick was very inquisitive and talkative as a child. He always wanted to try new things so that he could add to his experiences. His mother remembered him wanting to join the Boy Scouts. He asked her about it several times and wanted to know how he could get involved with the organisation. She registered him, but he changed his mind soon after the Scoutmaster had come over to meet him. While Sylvia may have been upset that Nick chose not to join after all the fuss, she respected his final decision.

Nick attended Silverstream Junior School then moved on to receive part of his education at Woodrush High School. As soon as Nick received seven O' levels, he left school. He never had any plans to attend college because he wanted to get out and start to experience the real world. Nick felt that he had the skills which would get him through life, and he wanted to put them to use as soon as possible.

His strong work ethic proved that he would be willing to do what was necessary in order to make a life for himself. As a child, he constantly looked for chores to do around the home, such as mowing the lawn, so that he could earn some extra money. Nick knew that his ambition and drive would get him far, but little did he know about the great success which was to reach him in a little less than three years' time.

This bright young man was no stranger to great music, and he was all for the big changes in sound that were occurring all around him in England's musical scene. As I have mentioned before, David Bowie's popularity was spreading, and it helped Nick establish a sense of direction in life, which would soon lead him to his own, great fame. Nick had an extensive record collection as a teenager, including many Bryan Ferry / Roxy Music and David Bowie albums.

His mother maintained that he had the largest Bowie collection in the whole country, and she grew tired of him constantly playing all his favourite records. He and John would race to the record store and see what they could find to purchase. It was a friendly competition that the two of them had shared. Also, according to Sylvia, Nick was a real packrat; he kept ticket stubs from every concert he attended.

While Nick and his mother were close and got along very well, one could not overrule the possibility of a rebellious adolescent. Nick says he can recall the first time that he had his hair coloured. He had naturally brown hair, but he came home with it blond one day, and he tried to avoid his mother, who was sitting downstairs. She saw him try to sneak by, and she went up to his room because she had her suspicions.

When she entered his room the next morning, he was still hiding under his blankets. Sylvia saw him come out of hiding as she spotted his blond head poking out of the covers. Even during his teens, Nick was no stranger to dying his hair to colours beyond blond. He also experimented with orange and purple, even before his days of stardom.

Needless to say, his mother was quite disappointed, but his hair colour was only one of the things they argued about over time. Nick and Sylvia were known to have strong arguments from time to time. There are so many things that could have been a lot worse than a little hair dye, though.

Nick didn't have any siblings, but he spent time with his two cousins, Annette and Colette Judd, during his childhood. Being that Nick was an only child, he grew close to his cousin, Colette, who is eight years his junior. He thought of her as the little sister he never had. Nick recalled the two of them being able to relate well and talk about anything that crossed their minds. She was a little different from Nick in the respect that she took her schooling seriously, and, at the age of thirteen, she was already thinking about what universities she would like to attend in the future.

She was also proud of his success and is glad that she is able to be a big part of his life. Collette was around the same age as the average Duranie at the time. Of course, she had an automatic bias for the band because her "brother" was one of the founding members. Although Nick was close to his cousins, not much was revealed about them in any formal news about the band.

Since Nick has always loved music, he found that he held an interest for the same artists that John had liked. John didn't have to second-guess his best friend because Nick liked the idea of being the co-founder of the band, so John was more than happy to recruit him as the second member.

At his young age, Nick had an air of sophistication when it came to music, although he had little formal training and education in the area. Nick's aforementioned dislike of school probably had something to do with that. The two of them collaborated on their ideas, and it was not long until they held practice sessions in Nick's parents' toy store, Bates' Toy Corner.

This is where they got the idea for one of their early song titles, "Hold Me, Pose Me," which they sung as an early demo, but the song never made it onto any of the band's albums. They had gotten the idea from the writing on a package of a stretchable toy doll. It further served as an example of their creative minds and strong writing abilities at work. The Bates' toy store had become a popular place for them to experiment with their music, and they did so most every opportunity they had, especially as more people came to join the band.

Now that some of the hard parts had already been taken care of; the concept, the band members, and a place for them to rehearse, all they had to do was think of a name. That sounded like their simplest task to date. It took them a little while, as they had thought of many names to call their group.

John had first contributed the name RAF as a possible suggestion, then he came up with a few others, but none of them stuck. John then brought his focus back to RAF because it was the most promising of all the choices at the time. While he and Nick may have thought that the name was interesting, they felt that it would not do much for them — the band definitely needed a better name.

Finally, the day for their destined name eventually came while the two of them were having beers in a pub, engaged in a conversation about movies. When the 1968 science fiction film *Barbarella*, starring Jane Fonda, came up in their conversation, they thought it would hold some definite possibilities. The two of them talked about the movie for a bit while they thought of more names for the band.

Then John got the idea by remembering the villain, Durand Durand, played by Milo O' Shea. John suggested that they name themselves after the strange character. Nick immediately found that he liked the idea; it certainly beat RAF, anyway. *What could it hurt?* they thought. So it was decided that their band would be called Duran Duran, deciding to drop the d on the end of each name in the process.

While *Barbarella* may be considered one of those cheesy sci-fi movies from the sixties, it was enough to provide this great band with a catchy name.

Barbarella was directed by Roger Vadim. The plot consists of Barbarella's character carrying out the orders of earth, searching for a missing astronaut named Durand Durand. Playing the part of a female James Bond, which may have caught John's interest, she eventually finds this Durand Durand, who turns out to be evil and essentially tries to destroy everything around him.

The film, based on a popular comic book series, contains themes of love, beauty, cruelty, and sexual pleasure, with bits of humour placed in between. The movie's soundtrack consists of strange but interesting music, which is mostly psychedelic in nature but not far off from something that the earliest line-up of Duran Duran could have produced.

****

John started out by playing guitar for the band, and Nick played synthesizer. They had a drum machine which provided rhythms, such as Rumba and Foxtrot, to be set to the songs. The rhythms were limited, but Nick worked with what he had. Both John and Nick practiced many songs and ideas together, but they knew they were still missing more members for their band.

It was not long after when they started putting these new beginnings into place and recruited additional members. First, to join was Stephen Duffy, who became their lead singer.

Steve and Nick took a liking to one another right away, and they wrote many songs during the time that they rehearsed at Bates' Toy Corner.

The first "album" which John, Nick, and Steve recorded in Bates'

In The Beginning

Toy Corner was entitled *Dusk and Dawn*. The cover art featured a streetscape shot of cars driving up and down Park Avenue, along with a picture of the three of them. The six songs are "Soundtrack," "Aztec Moon Rich," "Take (the Lines and the Shadows), "Hold Me/Pose Me," "A Lucien Melody," and "Hawks Don't Share."

Simon Colley soon joined, playing bass and clarinet. The foursome became the first official version of Duran Duran, and they started playing gigs wherever anyone would let them perform.

They started by playing some clubs in Birmingham, and one of the hottest spots in town was a place called Barbarella's. Sadly, the club was demolished in 2000.

Many early listeners at the club said that Duran Duran sounded a bit like Soft Cell, who came to prominence in the early eighties, but that changed as soon as Stephen Duffy and Simon Colley left the band. After all, Duran Duran was still experimenting with their sound.

In fact, Nick recalled one of Duran Duran's earliest gigs when they played in front of a punk crowd whose rough temperament suggested that the band would be less than welcome up on the stage. Stephen went up to the microphone and introduced a song that they had written, "So Cold in El Dorado," which was a tribute to F. Scott Fitzgerald.

Nick remembered panicking in his mind because he didn't know how the crowd was going to react to them. Surprisingly, the audience liked their performance, and as a result of a thunderous ovation, the band received their first ever encore.

During this time, however, there were those who thought that the band showed no promise, and they were less than confident in Duran Duran's abilities. The situation didn't look promising and both Duffy and Colley said that they wanted to move in separate directions.

Nick and John were surprised and disappointed by the news, but they knew they had to respect their wishes and let them leave the band. Simon Colley headed off in more of a rock 'n' roll direction, while Stephen Duffy went solo, adding Tin Tin to his name. A couple of his solo hits included the songs "Kiss Me" and "Hold Me." During the late 1980s, Duffy changed his sound and became involved with a band called Lilac Tune.

He later released several solo albums under his name. Some of them include, *The Ups and Downs* (1985), *Because We Love You* (1986), *Designer Beatnik* (1986), *Music in Colours* (1993), *Duffy*

(1995), *I Love My Friends* (1998), *They Called Him Tin Tin* (1998).

Colley's solo work after Duran Duran consisted of forming a band called Subterranean Hawks with Steven Duffy and two former members of a group called TV Eye. They were very short-lived, and no one has heard much from Simon Colley since the breakup of this other band. Nick remarked that Colley became a chef.

After Duffy and Colley left the band, a new vocalist by the name of Andy Wickett stepped in. His previous experience included singing for TV Eye, the band having taken its name from an Iggy and The Stooges song. Wickett had formed the band in 1976 with Eamon Duffy and Dave Kusworth. It was the same band that Colley and Duffy formed Subterranean Hawks with the other two members of.

Wickett's music and flamboyant dress sense was influenced by the New York Dolls. Soon after he joined the band, Nick's rhythm box started proving itself to be unreliable, with only a limited amount of sound.

Nick had been only too aware of this and it was no longer capable of producing the sounds that the band wanted. Duran Duran needed a drummer who could provide rhythms that were more varied than the ones coming from his machine.

It wasn't much later when Andy attended a party and found himself in the company of a young James Dean look-alike who went by the name of Roger Taylor. Andy was drunk, and he explained that Duran Duran was in need of a drummer. When Roger said that he was interested, Andy invited him to audition for the band.

With the help of Andy, Roger Taylor was incorporated into Duran Duran. The other members found it to be a great improvement because Roger was, indeed, a skilled musician who proved himself to be the solid backbone of the band. He proved his musical talent, and ensured himself a solid spot with Duran Duran, therefore cementing its sound and longevity.

Roger Andrew Taylor was born on April 26, 1960 at Heathville Hospital in Birmingham, near Castle Bromwich. He was the second son born to Jean and Hughie Taylor. Roger grew up on a farm with a loving family consisting of his parents and his older brother, Stephen, and two younger sisters.

He was very quiet as a child and often hid himself in the back of the classroom at school. He had gone through Castle Bromwich Junior School and Park Hall School without any bad incidents and graduated

In The Beginning

with excellent passing grades. He was the good child whom every parent hoped to have.

His mother wasn't upset that Roger had no plans to attend college, but she didn't care for the way he coveted a rock star's life. Jean didn't think it was a realistic career path for her son. Roger's father also hoped he would pursue a career in the auto industry, but his son seemed to want no part of that because he already had his goal set in his mind.

Roger always liked music from an early age. He recalls some of his favourites being similar to what others in the band were interested in. The first record he bought was the Jackson Five's hit single, "ABC," when he was ten years old. The group was one of his favourites at the time.

Oddly enough, he doesn't remember getting his next record until a few years later, probably around the time he was fifteen. The record was by the Alex Harvey Band. Some of his later musical influences proved to assist him when he was looking for similarities that he shared with his new friends. Roger also cited Genesis as one of his biggest musical influences.

Roger was passionate about water sports, which earned him the nickname Froggy with the other members of the band. He liked swimming and diving in particular.

Of course, he's also always had a great affinity for playing music. Roger's mother recalled that when he was young, he incessantly banged away at the empty milk bottles he used as drums, using her knitting needles as sticks. She joked that it used to drive her crazy, but she admitted it paid off in the long run since she knew that he got to fulfil his dream. This is just another example of Roger's future stardom in its early stages, and the rest of the world had yet to know of its greatest ability.

By the time Roger was fifteen, he was already playing in a few different bands. It is also said that a lot of the bands had weird names. One of the most popular of these was Crucified Toad, which probably got its name from the short-lived, early seventies music fanzine.

Another band in which he played was known as the Scent Organs, which was commonly mislabelled as the Sex Organs, much to his mother's dismay. Roger joined Scent Organs when he was seventeen. The band would rotate their practice sessions back and forth in each other's bedrooms, and Roger's parents were not too thrilled when it was their turn to house these sessions. He experimented with different sounds, thus building up the experience that would allow him to become an essential part of Duran Duran.

Just like many people who are interested in music, Roger had idols during his childhood and early teens. He said that he would have liked to have met Yes's lead singer Jon Anderson because their music had inspired him greatly.

Roger also had his great moment of pre fame when he got to meet one of his greatest idols, David Bowie. He still fondly looks back on the experience with stars in his eyes and remembers it as being one of the greatest moments of his life. If nothing else had led him to want to become famous, then this incident was something that probably pushed him to want to taste the spotlight.

When he received the invitation to join Duran Duran, Roger found that he had the same musical tastes as Nick and John. They all shared the same love for punk artists such as The Cure, Siouxsie Sioux and the Banshees and, of course, David Bowie — The perfect chemistry to formulate their ideas.

Their productivity in putting their thoughts together was pushing them into the direction that would shape the recognisable Duran Duran sound. They also had the urge to produce the same kind of sound that had helped David Bowie achieve his extraordinary level of fame.

By 1979 this second version of Duran Duran was proving to be more successful. The band began to record a demo tape, which consisted of four songs; "Girls on Film," "Dreaming of Your Cars," — most likely an idea of John's — "Reincarnation," and a song title that Nick couldn't remember at the time but is called "Working the Steel." The demo tape was produced by Bob Lamb, a former drummer for Steve Gibbons, in a home studio he had built in one of his rooms.

It was not long after that when Andy Wickett left the band, to be replaced by Jeff Thomas from Roger's former band, the Scent Organs. He was hired because the other members thought that he was a John Fox sound alike. John Taylor decided to trade his guitar for a bass, which left room for a guitarist to join the band. This posed the problem of finding someone to take over. Just as before, Duran Duran had the persistence to move on.

Alan Curtis got the lead guitarist role. He was recruited after he replied to a magazine ad that called for someone fitting the description of a guitarist for a Roxy/Bowie influenced band. They liked his music,

In The Beginning

and he was hired to fill the position.

They made two more demos, which were called "Enigmatic Swimmers," and "See Me, Repeat Me," the latter whose name strikes a resemblance to the earlier practice demo, "Hold Me, Pose Me." Interestingly enough, parts of "See Me, Repeat Me" were converted into certain elements that made up *Rio*.

Of the demos, obviously "Girls on Film" went on to become a No.1 selling single and one of the band's greatest songs. The others had not been placed on any of their albums, nor have they ever been released to the public, as of yet. While this is a sad truth, it is the fact of the matter, and these songs are merely memories of something that were made before the band reached their fame.

Duran Duran was back to the point at which they started, and it appeared as though they were not making much progress. The band was still evolving, but it seemed as though it would never stabilise. The fact that in such a short space of time band members had come and gone certainly concerned John and Nick, but they were not going to be deterred — they had to finish what they started, regardless of how the current situation seemed.

In February 1980 the band paid a visit to a classy disco joint in Birmingham called the Rum Runner, which was demolished in 1987. Their very first shows at the night club consisted of a set list of a few songs. These songs were played at nearly every show until 1985. It was there that they met the owners of the establishment, two brothers named Paul and Michael Berrow.

The Berrow brothers took a liking to the band almost immediately and wanted to hear more of their work. The two brothers, however, didn't like new vocalist Jeff Thomas, and the feeling was mutual. They soon got the idea to take the band under their wing and became their managers.

The Berrows were responsible for managing Duran Duran in their early days while shaping their line-up and image, essentially catering to the likes of their current audience. The members of the band also took up some extra jobs at the night club to earn a little more money on the side. They needed to keep up with their costs and expenses so that the band could continue performing. Roger cleared tables and cleaned out bar glasses, while Nick took on the job of a D.J.

Alan Curtis got along with the other members and had no problem collaborating with them on their ideas. He supported their work while they performed at Barbarella's, but he left shortly after the band started playing at the Rum Runner. He followed the footsteps of Stephen Duffy and Andy Wickett to pursue other goals.

In lieu of Duran Duran's recent troubles of trying to find a new guitarist, the Berrows decided to place an ad in *Melody Maker*. Compared to the previous ad citing Roxy/Bowie influence that had secured Curtis's services, now the ad was more specific:

LEAD
RHYTHM
GUITARIST
(Ronson, Manzanera, Gilmour)
Stylish/powerful/inventive to join band
with financially strong management

Many guys applied, but no one seemed to set off fireworks in the band until a nineteen-year-old from Newcastle, Andrew Taylor, came along. He had enough confidence in his ability to assure himself that he was going to be invited to join the band. Besides, he thought if the other guys didn't like his music, they would be missing out on one of the greatest talents that they had ever witnessed.

Although there may have been some misinforming rumours that the three Taylors are brothers, it has long been confirmed that none of them are related. Taylor, after all, is a very common surname.

At his audition, Duran Duran and the Berrows thought Andy was perfect for the band, especially since he said he didn't object to dressing up and wearing makeup, although he didn't really mean it. Andy thought that was what the other members of the band would want him to do, so he made up his mind to please them.

Even though most members of the band primarily got along, Andy and Nick were notorious for butting heads ever since they met. Nick soon found that he didn't care too much for Andy's casual attire. In fact, Nick was a bit hesitant about letting him into the band because he didn't like his jeans. Andy felt that Nick's style of dressing in fancy clothing and wearing excessive amounts of makeup was to the other extreme.

Andy was born on February 16, 1961 in Tynemouth Royal Infirmary and was the first child to Ron and Blanche Taylor. He later had one younger brother, Ron. Andy was very close to and protective of his younger brother. He also eventually had two stepsisters. Sometimes, he fought to protect his brother when bullies used to tease him in school. During his teen years, Andy was known for being a scrapper, and he often found himself getting into fights, which was probably part of the reason he had earned the "tough guy" label in the band.

Ron was a fisherman, and the family was raised in a poor environment. They didn't have the standard conveniences that most average families took for granted. As a result of their poverty, the Taylors had to use an outhouse and bathe outside in a tin tub. Since Andy's father and grandfather were both men of the sea, they hoped that Andy would become a fisherman. He declined their offer, however, and thought about working in carpentry, that is, until he had his rock 'n' roll epiphany.

Andy was an extremely bright child, and he had done well in all his courses and excelled in mathematics. Even at a young age, he found that his mind worked good with numbers. He had also taken an interest in playing soccer during his youth.

Regrettably, when Andy was eleven, he came home from school one day to find that his mother had packed up and left the family. Just when things seemed bad enough as they were, Ron ended up having to raise both children by himself.

Things seemed to move in a more positive direction when Ron bought Andy an electric guitar for Christmas that same year. While his father encouraged him to play the guitar, he didn't necessarily want him to aspire to become a pop star. Ron was a practical man, and he passed that trait on to his son.

By the time Andy turned thirteen, he became interested in wanting to take guitar lessons. The enthusiastic lad recalled when he began to take lessons from a guy across the road named Dave Black, who charged £1 per session. Many would probably agree that no one, not even Andy, really knew the significance of these guitar lessons and how they would impact his future.

Dave also helped Andy out by getting him an audition with a local cover band that played at working men's clubs in Northern England. Also, to help out his family a little, Andy paid his father rent with the money he had received from playing in the band. He thought it would be the right thing to do since money was tight.

Andy left school when he was sixteen and started to embark upon his musical career. The next band in which he played was a punk outfit who called themselves The Gigolos, but they soon renamed themselves Motorway.

In 1977, A&M became interested in the band, and they gave them a single deal, which allowed Motorway to produce and release their first and only single, "Teenage Girls." When Andy found out that the single wasn't going to get the band very far, he lost interest in their work. Soon after that, Motorway disbanded as they could see that things weren't going to pan out for them.

Shortly after, a local punk contest was held, and a band by the name of Ward 34, were the winners. The person who promoted the contest was supposed to record the winners' music in his studio, but he had other commitments that prevented him from doing so.

Andy was offered the job, and he was delighted at having gained the opportunity to "make music from the other side." The chance to produce was another great experience that helped him along the way. After his brief recording stint, Andy played in a large number of bands and performed around six hundred shows before he joined Duran Duran. This included the thirteen months he played throughout Germany, and ten weeks after that, he performed at a Greek beach club.

His time in Germany was gruelling, but Andy thought it to be a valuable experience because it taught him how to perform and work with other musicians. He soon ran into problems, however, and felt that he didn't work very well with these bands. Andy came to the conclusion that he would take his talent elsewhere and find someone with whom he could better relate. Then, it was only a matter of time before he found them.

CHAPTER 2

The Man in the Pink Leopard Skin Trousers

In 1980, a young lady by the name of Fiona Kemp, who was a barmaid at the Rum Runner, changed the face of Duran Duran forever. Fiona heard that the band was looking for a new lead singer, so she decided to recommend a friend of hers, Simon Le Bon.

She and Simon dated for a while when he was in college, but they had split up by this time. Fiona didn't let that affect her choice as she thought he would be perfect for the job. She told the enthusiastic Simon, who eagerly phoned Michael Berrow and made arrangements to meet with Nick and Roger the next day. Essentially, the experimentation that had gone on before ceased when Simon joined the band. Their sound had changed so much during those first two years.

The band took a great liking to him instantly, even though they initially thought he was a bit weird. Nick in particular liked his outfit. Simon's attire consisted of pink leopard skin trousers, a brown suede jacket, cowboy boots, and sunglasses, a far cry from Nick's Bowie-influenced style.

Nick also liked the book that Simon had with him because it had interesting drawings and the band's name scrawled all over the front. His notebook was filled with songs and lyrics such as "Underneath the Clocktower," "On a Dead Child," "Night Boat," and "The Chauffeur."

Another poem was called "Tel Aviv," whose title was included as the last track on their first album, but all the words had been taken out. Years later when the song was made public on the Internet, fans were treated to the jazzy instruments which accompanied the poem. The original "Tel Aviv" recalled Simon's days in Israel. Many would argue the original version is just as good, if not better than the one featured on the album.

The other members of the band played backup tracks for his lyrics.

Simon only had to listen to them twice before he formulated the idea for and wrote "The Sound of Thunder," which he had performed with the band shortly after beginning to work with them.

The song was considered celebratory for Simon after making it into the band. It makes sense if one pays close attention to the lyrics. When Simon sang, he did so with such charisma and everyone was impressed with his vocal range and talent.

It seemed as though he had been a natural for this kind of performing, and his voice proved his claim. Of course, from then on, there was no question that he was surely going to be Duran Duran's new lead singer because he had what they were looking for.

Simon John Charles Le Bon was born on October 27, 1958 and was the first son of John and Ann Le Bon. Simon also shared his birthday with his father. He was born in Bushey, Hertfordshire. His family members are descendants of the French Huguenots — Protestants who fled to England in the sixteenth century to escape persecution from Catholic France.

The Le Bon family hailed from Normandy, and if anyone is interested in looking up the family coat of arms, it is said to be located in the Huguenot crypt in Canterbury Cathedral in England.

Simon's parents did their best to make a good life for their son. Simon says that his earliest memory is of him lying in his crib and being visited by the cat that his family owned. He also recalled being mesmerised by the things that hung over him in the crib as he reached his hands out to try and touch the fascinating objects.

Simon was very precocious, and his mother recalls him having started to gain an interest in the arts at a very young age. Simon was only a little over two when he started to recite poems. His mother would write them for him so that they would be preserved. It was not long after when he began writing them down for himself.

As his mind grew, so did his love for literature. A lot of his literary talent could very well have come from his mother, who had written a series of children's books that were based on Simon as a child. Unfortunately, if they are not out of print, they are very difficult to find.

His two younger brothers are David and John, who are sometimes shown in articles about the band and in Simon's childhood photos. Simon grew up in what he calls a "total middle-class home," and he has fond memories of his childhood. He was especially fond of his mother, who used to dote on him. As a child, nearly every time she left him, he used to sit by the window and cry until she returned home to him.

Ann was an actress, who had to give up her career for the benefit of her marriage. What she wanted for herself she transferred to Simon. When he was five, she started taking him to auditions for acting commercials. As a child, Simon appeared in a commercial for Persil laundry detergent, which was supposed to clean the stain out of his dirty shirt. He also did advertisements for Coca-Cola and a French coffee manufacturer.

His early interest in male modelling came into play when he modelled knitwear clothes for a women's magazine. Simon had come from a background rich in show business. His grandmother had been one of the original Tiller Girls, a famous performing group at the time, and his great aunt had the honour of dancing before the Queen with a very famous group called the Ziegfeld Follies.

Simon was afraid of demons as a child, so he put toy soldiers on his window. He thought they would protect him from nightmares while he slept. He also had a favourite companion with whom he spent most of his time, a teddy bear called Shockermoler, who apparently had a sour disposition. The bear's tough image, consisting of an eye patch and a safety pin through one of his ears, proved in Simon's mind to be his best protector.

When Simon was about six or seven, his mother also enrolled him in the Boy Scouts. The young Mr. Le Bon was excited about becoming a part of the organisation. He had a good time at the initial part of the meeting, but he left after the first day because he claimed that the other boys were mean. They ridiculed Simon, which brought him close to tears, and one had even kicked him. Needless to say, any future plans involving the Boy Scouts were over.

Simon always enjoyed music and singing when he was young, his earliest singing experience was in his church choir. Mr. Turvey, the church organist, would accompany his voice. His mother had recorded him singing "He Shall Feed His Flock," part of Händel's *Messiah*. Simon also sang a few other songs.

Although many would say that it was an enriching experience for Simon, he claims that he didn't like his voice back then. He made the assertion that it is painful to hear how his voice sounded during that time. Ann, however, was extremely proud that he was in the choir.

Unfortunately, the recording was never made public, so one can only imagine how Simon sounded during those formative days of his singing career. His mother worried about the strain he was putting on his voice in singing so many songs for the church. As a result, she withdrew him from the choir. It was not until Fiona Kemp urged him to resume singing, by encouraging him to audition for the band, that he changed his mind.

During his early adolescence, Simon won several cups and medals for his outstanding poetry, which would later become known to many of his fans. This was where his talent of reciting poetry at a very early age started to pay off and made his mother very proud of his accomplishments.

Aside from his music, I am not sure how many poems he has written, but some of them are included in various books and articles published about the band. One of his most intriguing works is a poem called "A Strange Encounter," which describes the narrator's encounter with a supernatural being. Later during his career, he also recorded two more of his poems, "God," and "This Is How a Road Gets Made." They are currently available on CD No.6 of the band's second box set.

Even though Simon was not very fond of his schooling, he had an excellent education and has always had an inclination toward the arts. The schools he attended included West Lodge Primary School and Pinner Grammar School (Elton John had also gone there) before moving on to Harrow Art College, and then Birmingham University.

Even though he found himself distracted during many of his classes, Simon's teachers said that he excelled in the arts so much — clearly his strongest point. He achieved the highest grades in Art and English.

Be all this as it may, Simon was still not without vice. He had lived some rebellious days in his youth by experimenting with alcohol and drugs. His wild experiences became a major part of his youth. There was also one funny story when he and some of his friends went off one night to see a concert. They ended up missing the last bus home. Simon recalled that they eventually found a man who let them spend the night in his bathroom.

When he got home the next day, he had told his mother —who had spent the entire night worried sick — that they had to sleep on paper towels on the floor. It was a cold winter night, so they used a broom to prop the hand dryer so that it stayed on all night to keep themselves warm!

In 1977, he joined a punk band called Dog Days, whose performances were limited to shows at Harrow Technical College. Both the band and the shows, however, ended abruptly in 1978. Simon described his experience of playing at the college as interesting. He also recalled things such as the band having to play on the floor and having their microphones turned off for going over the time limit.

Simon laughed when he remembered that he went to the other microphones when his was shut off. After the performances their time would be spent in the pub. The typical way for Simon to celebrate before he reached great fame. The only thing that may have changed, in this respect, are the people with whom he celebrated with. Simon was always a lover of music. The first rock concert he attended was on Genesis' *The Lamb Lies Down on Broadway* Tour.

Before joining Duran Duran, Simon had some very interesting jobs, to say the least. His first "real" job was as a porter at Northwick Park Hospital in Harrow. Some of the things he saw were naturally quite disturbing to him, such as severed limbs and dead bodies.

While these things were certainly unnerving, he thought that he worked in a good atmosphere because the will to survive was abundant in those who were being hospitalised. A short while before he went on to college, Simon spent some time working on a kibbutz in Israel. While he was there, he learned numerous skills, such as lumberjacking, tractor driving, orange picking, and looking after children.

Simon loved his experience in Israel. It was close to paradise because he only worked four hours a day, and the rest he dedicated to his leisure time. This was when he got the opportunity to sunbathe while showing off his body to interested girls. It was an overall enjoyable experience.

Simon enrolled at Birmingham University, in Edgbaston, for one year to study acting. He also applied to drama schools such as RADA and Bristol Old Vic, but his applications were promptly denied. Acting was something of which he was very fond, but he dropped out of college to pursue his career in music.

Simon admits that part of his love for drama started at a young age, when he craved a lot of attention. This goes back to when he used to cry for his mother when she left him at home. Along the same lines, Simon also admitted that he was greatly fascinated by women. When he was around eight or nine, he had his first crush on an older girl named Alison. Simon joked that he acted a bit like a stalker because he remembers following her nearly everywhere she went. And, although he was a bit shy, he wanted that girl to take notice of him.

As the years continued, so did his fascination for different girls. Many girls at his college also became interested in him because of his acting, and he admits that is why he stuck with it for a time.

Later, when Simon grew closer to his band mates, he had affectionately been called by the popular version of his middle name, Charlie. This started when Simon Cook, joined as a crew member and started calling him by that name because Andy was getting confused by having two Simons in the band. This also began to stick with many of his fans, who began to call him by his designated nickname.

CHAPTER 3

Heyday

Now that Duran Duran had all their pieces fall into place they started to take off in a direction that would make famous around the world.

Michael Berrow did his best to support them in any way that he could. He mortgaged his house to raise money so that he could get the support slot on Hazel O'Conner's first proper UK tour.

O'Conner recalled how her manager had talked about the possibility of this new band from Birmingham opening the shows and being happy to pay a 'buy on' (a fee to get on a big tour, as it gives huge exposure to new artists). It helped that Hazel O'Connor liked their music.

In fact, every night she would nip out into the concert hall to catch one of their songs. The favourite with herself and her band was "Planet Earth".

She also recalled that the lads wore a fair amount of frilly shirts, which didn't always go down so well with her punk audience. But O'Connor thought they had a great attitude and were undaunted by the punk jibes.

They had so little money in their tour budget, that they travelled in a camper van. Each night they'd get one room in the hotel that O'Connor's band and crew stayed at, and then pull straws to see who got the room.

They also got to hang out at the hotel after the gigs with Hazel O'Connor and her entourage. Simon would ask O'Connor about the self-hypnosis she had been doing, and he enquired if it would help if one was afraid of losing one's voice. She recalled that he was so intense and committed — indeed that all the Duran lads were — and O'Connor said that the two acts had so many brilliant times on that first tour together.

It certainly paid off and with those live performances, they won more fans than Spandau Ballet, who were seen as one of their biggest rivals during the 1980s.

Duran Duran's early life, however, was nothing near as glamorous as some may think. As previously stated, they spent several nights in campers and were paid very little for their performances. All was not lost, however and the best was yet to come. Duran Duran generated enough public interest to have record companies come and beat down those camper doors.

Business picked up, and they knew that everything was going to be all right and they would get a chance to fulfil their dreams. They were going to have their chance to take the world by storm.

In December 1980, Duran Duran got their first record deal with EMI Records. Shortly after, the band received a weekly allowance, which began to give them the financial support they needed. They no longer had to spend nights in their camper van. As part of their record deal, EMI allowed the guys to pick their own producer. They chose Colin Thurston and Red Bus Studios of London. It worked great with Colin helping them move in the direction they needed to go.

The same month they began to produce more songs, such as the ever famous "Planet Earth" and "Careless Memories" which gained exposure on BBC Radio 1. Tensions were rising as the band became very anxious to know just how well their songs had been doing. Luckily for them, by January 1981, "Planet Earth" had risen to No.12 on the charts. Also, the fact that they made an appearance on England's prime music show, *Top of the Pops*, helped raise the band's profile. Now the public could match their faces to their names. And since people liked them so much, Duran Duran was invited to make appearances on other television shows. More TV exposure increased their recognition and popularity.

Their first self-titled album came out in February 1981, and their first single, "Planet Earth," generated a great amount of success. It was released in stores on February 2. By the end of the year, it reached No.1 on the charts in Sweden, Portugal, and Australia. Unfortunately, "Careless Memories" had not done so well because it only made it to No.37. But that did not deter the band — this was the merely the beginning of something truly great.

Shortly after, the band headed to the United States to start their first tour, which was well-received. They had a good start toward

Heyday

making their dreams come true, but the album had not done as well as they would have liked. Some say that their first effort, essentially, was a failure, but this was only the tip of the iceberg. Great things were still to come.

During the US tour they had the opportunity to meet and work with Andy Warhol. He was greatly fascinated with the band, and he invited them to his studio for a photo session. It may be common knowledge to most Duranies that he used to masturbate to some of their videos, especially "Girls on Film." It was also said that he was smitten with Nick. The starstruck artist wrote love letters to Nick, who did not take his bold declaration with a grain of salt.

On August 1, 1981, a new television dedicated music channel called MTV aired its first music video, "Video Killed the Radio Star" by The Buggles.

MTV was a huge hit with the youth in the 1980s because it was fresh and exciting, and the videos made with the music created a whole new medium. Young preteens and adolescent girls who watched the network didn't take long to find that they had fallen for Duran Duran's good looks and charm.

The New Romantic image showed off the band's pouty faces and pretty looks, which seemed to be all the rage in 1981. Once the young consumers saw the "product," the viewer ratings let the network know that Duran Duran was high in demand. The advent of MTV played a big part in the band's success because they played their videos to everyone in the United States.

Before MTV existed, Duran Duran had a limited audience because it was more difficult to reach people without the aid of their videos. Other popular singles from the band's first album include "Careless Memories" and "Girls on Film." The latter of the two, not surprisingly, caused enough controversy for the video to be banned from MTV, due to its racy content of titillating nude scenes. Finally, after a compromise, "Girls on Film" could be aired again without any of the nudity, so an edited version of the video was played on the channel.

The band knew they wanted to make videos, but they were not sure who they wanted to be their director. The band had a very important agenda, as they wanted to make sure their depth matched the images in their videos. This would ensure that the music would not just be going along with the beats.

The first three videos from songs off their debut album, *Duran*

Duran, were directed separately by three different men. "Planet Earth" was directed under television advertiser Russell Mulcahy. Terry Jones (not the one from *Monty Python*) and Perry Haines directed "Careless Memories." The infamous "Girls on Film" was directed by Kevin Godley and Lol Crème. All three videos were filmed in London. All the directors did well with the videos, and the members of the band felt that it was a good experience having worked with five people for three videos.

Russell helped the band's first video come to life by using a science fiction theme and the latest technology, which aimed to make it appear less dated. The second of the two, "Careless Memories," did less than thrill the band because of its icy, emotional distance.

Even though the band hoped to capture the true emotion of the song the directors liked the icy elements which the video portrayed. As many may probably already know, "Girls on Film" won the band both positive and negative acclaim after it was first viewed on the American late night dance club circuit.

In order to spice up the videos even more, Kevin Godley and Lol Crème shot scantily clad women while they took part in such activities as pillow fighting and mud wrestling. The Berrow brothers were on a mission to prove that Duran Duran was not a "gay band," as some critics used to refer to them.

They showed the long version of "Girls on Film" at many bars across the United States to prove their point. It was that same song, however, that placed Duran Duran's debut album at No.3 on the charts, resulting in sales totalling 1.6 million worldwide.

One video that I find very fascinating is "Night Boat," which could be described as a mini movie. In it, the band befalls the horrors of being pursued by zombies, who want to take them over. Simon is fascinated with this thing called the "night boat," and he finds himself being elsewhere mentally when his concerned band mates try to call his name.

During the scene in which he speaks, which may sound a little unintelligible to some, he is actually quoting Mercutio's soliloquy from Act I, Scene II of William Shakespeare's famous play, *Romeo and Juliet*. This is just a small example of the director's creativity at work.

Simon talked about the beginning of the video, as he made several references to a movie called *Summer of '42*. The film was made in

1971 and takes place on Nantucket Island. The plot consists of a young man who anticipates his first sexual encounter. He inadvertently falls in love with a woman who has yet to hear of her soldier husband's fate during the war.

"Night Boat," was shot at various dusty and rural locations. The band recorded some natural dialogue before they segued into their monologues. The video starts off with somewhat of an eerie tone, but it gets more bizarre as day fades into night. This allows for the coming of the night boat.

The deadly vessel delivered zombies, who attacked members of the band, giving the video a scary element, which may still give chills to some people today. Some may jokingly state that this is the reason that Nick doesn't like boats. (Actually, it's mostly because he has a fear of water.)

In various interviews, members of the band stated that if they could make it big in America, then they would have it made. Nothing was closer to the truth. MTV helped them immensely because they were one of the first bands who made videos. Even though most of them were low-budget, audiences found them captivating, and they wanted to see more.

The videos were what won Duran Duran the majority of their fame as they set the standard for other bands' videos, which were still undergoing production. The creativity in these videos allowed the band to excel as the audience found themselves captivated with the mini movies and the stories that they told.

They were also relieved that they could now shed their pretty boy, New Romantic image, which stuck with them for some time after the release of their first album. The band knew the image didn't suit them. They admitted that they only used it because they thought they needed it in order to succeed. Now that they had established themselves in the music industry, they could do whatever they pleased with their image. They took advantage of their new identity for their upcoming second album, *Rio*.

On November 16, 1981, "My Own Way" was only released as a single in the UK. It only reached No.14 on the UK charts and the lads regretted not pushing for worldwide released. They ended 1981 with their *Careless Memories* UK Tour. All seventeen shows were sold-out including two nights at Hammersmith Odeon and finishing with three gigs at Birmingham's venue of the same name.

Reach Up For The Sunrise

1982 was a big year for the band with the release of their second album, *Rio*, which probably still remains their most famous album. They decided that they didn't want their image on the cover and enlisted the talents of Patrick Nagel, who created the cover painting. Malcolm Garrett, who worked for Assorted Images, designed the album. What the band really wanted with their new theme was a girl that matched the image.

Patrick was known for his paintings of beautiful women, which were light years away from ordinary. The artist was renowned for the work that he did on celebrities, especially Joan Collins from television's *Dynasty*.

Patrick's talents had earned him recognition as a post Warhol painter, which caught the interest of the band. He was more than honoured to undergo the task of creating the new album cover, which served as a great visual to the band's fame. The job he did on the cover was so spectacular that the band wanted to hand out copied prints of the painting, but they figured that the cost would set them back too much.

Unfortunately, Patrick passed away in 1984 at the young age of thirty-eight. His work, however, will continue to live on.

Rio helped the band see its first success in the United States. As well as reaching No.2 in the UK, it also earned the same spot on the American charts. With unforgettable singles such as "Hungry Like the Wolf," and "Rio," the band captured the hearts of many young girls, who would become Duran Duran's most loyal fans. (This was around the same time I was introduced to the videos for "Rio" and "Hungry Like the Wolf.") "Hungry Like the Wolf" placed at No.5 on the charts on the 4th May.

When asked what inspired the song, Simon replied that it was brought on by Jim Morrison. Of course, Simon also said that "Rio" was about a girl. There is also the popular explanation that the song celebrates the beauty of America, especially pertaining to the areas in the southwest.

The album was recorded at Air Studios, on Oxford Street, London's busiest shopping street. Air stood for "Associated Independent Recording." The establishment was founded by former Beatles' producer Sir George Martin, along with John Burgess. Paul McCartney was recording in the studio next door to theirs, popped in to listen to "Rio" and gave Duran Duran a thumbs up to show his approval.

"Rio" was the video that had sealed their fame. It gained them the recognition they had strove to attain in the United States. Although Duran Duran was considered a teen-based group, their appeal expanded to other age groups as well.

"Rio" was filmed in Antigua. The song was written to describe the beauty of America, the very same beauty that captivated Duran Duran during their first trip to the country and conveyed through the video.

During the filming of "Rio," Andy was accidentally thrown off the side of the boat much to his chagrin, even though the footage remained in the video.

Filmed in exotic Sri Lanka, the videos for "Hungry Like the Wolf," "Save a Prayer," and "Lonely in Your Nightmare" were done on a low budget of £45,000. Even though that was the case, the videos were, and still are, enchanting all the same.

"Hungry Like the Wolf" was matched up with *Raiders of the Lost Ark*, which came out only one year earlier. People can compare the video to the movie because of the clothing Simon wears and the tasks he undergoes to lustily pursue the woman, as portrayed by model Sheila Ming.

Getting to film these videos in such exotic locations was not all it was cracked up to be. They were appalled by the unsanitary manner in which some food was sold, strung up in the open.

Simon and Nick vowed that they weren't going to eat it and not many people would blame them. They also avoided tap water to avoid getting any diseases.

Aside from the malaria infestations in the area and the illnesses the band members suffered, they also recalled having some problems with their fellow animal stars in the video. John remembers, as he described, "having the privilege of an elephant relieving itself all over me," which must have been one of the most unpleasant things he had experienced during the filming.

The video filming for "Save a Prayer" took place in the holy city of Anuradhapura before travelling on to the highlands of Kandy, where they were anything but welcome. The natives didn't want outsiders on their sacred Buddhist sites, and they were faced with threats of being arrested or worse, killed while filming the video.

Roger also had another encounter with an elephant although this time it was quite scary. Roger was seated on the back of a male elephant, who picked up the scent of a nearby female on heat. The amorous animal then rushed down the river, with Roger hanging on for dear life as the male mounted the female!

Roger remembered it as being, "the most frightening experience of my life." Despite the unsettling experiences that he had in Sri Lanka, Roger named it as one of his favourite places in the world, with Australia trailing close behind.

It had taken the band a while to recover from the illnesses they caught in Sri Lanka. Andy had not yet completely recovered, and he collapsed after a performance in Australia the following March. He suffered from a disease called pyrexia, which included symptoms of fatigue and self-neglect. He also unknowingly swam in some water that was infected with urine from one of the elephants. As a result of Andy's illness, their European tour dates had to be postponed, and *Rio* was released without an immediate tour to back it up.

Duran Duran, in many ways, had been compared to the sixties British phenomenon who had started it all, The Beatles. Besides the fact that both bands hailed from English cities, Duran Duran found that they had other similarities with the revolutionary band who started the British rock 'n' roll invasion.

Duran Duran played up to the comparisons with their sixties predecessors. Nick recalls joking that the band was going to one day make a movie called *Yelp!*, which would be a parody of The Beatles' famous film, *Help!* They also enjoyed the fact that they had the ability to make girls scream.

Nick recalled playing to hysterical audiences, who lost control even more when the lads came on stage or did something to generate such a reaction. The band, sometime later, also acquired the label "The Fab Five" during the height of their fame. This, to an extent, paralleled The Beatles' previous label as "The Fab Four."

The Fab Five's early line-up on tour was bolstered with Andy Hamilton, who played saxophone, and two female backup singers by the names of B.J. Nelson and Charmaine Burch.

Duran Duran appeared to have it all, especially when they toured the world and met many girls. Andy was the first one to fall in love; he was smitten with the band's hairdresser, Tracey Wilson. Her family owned the appropriately named barbering business Wilson, Wilson & Wilson. Andy and Tracey were married, on July 31, 1982, breaking the hearts of the young ladies who were infatuated with him.

Heyday

He admitted to having many girls in his life before, but he said that Tracey was the one who made him feel the best. Andy was a fast mover, and he felt that he was ready to settle down. Despite his young age, he wanted to marry the woman he loved.

His proposal had been less than conventional. On February 16, 1982, Andy's twenty-first birthday, he planned to go out and celebrate, but Tracey didn't join him because she was feeling ill. When he came in from partying, nearly at four in the morning, he asked her if she wanted to marry him. At first, she thought it was one of his jokes, but she accepted his proposal the next morning.

Unfortunately, Tracey's parents could not be with her to join in the celebration because of business obligations. The wedding took place in Los Angeles, and the whole band attended the ceremony.

The Berrow brothers, Roger, and John contributed to the wedding finances to for the couple's special day. The band all dressed in suitable attire for a celebrity wedding with top hats, morning coats, pearl tiepins, and pinstripe trousers.

A nervous John was Andy's best man. One of the most unique gifts the couple was given was a cigarette-pack-shaped lighter from Nick. They also received a porcelain sake set Simon had picked up during the band's tour of Japan.

After the two were married, Tracey had taken Taylor as her last name, and Andy made Wilson his middle name since he previously didn't have one of his own. Tracey has had a phenomenal impact on Andy, as she has encouraged him to cut down on his spending and lead an overall healthier life.

This was one of the things that made Tracey special to him, and he loved her even more for introducing him to a healthier and happier lifestyle. The couple is still happily married, nearly forty years on, and they have four children; Andy Taylor Jr., Bethany, Georgiana, and Isabelle.

Duran Duran made a name for themselves worldwide, but their fame came with a bit of a price. Unfortunately, not everything was always as fun and carefree as it seemed. The troubles the band encountered were not only narrow escapes from fans who had gotten too close, but they also had some "foes" to deal with, as well.

The only public attack made on anyone in the group was when a man accused Roger of stealing his drink. Even though there are many variations concerning how the incident occurred, many people remember it as happening after a performance in Munich. The accuser leapt on Roger and kept beating him until he was rendered unconscious.

When Roger came to in the hospital, he found that he had stitches in his head and that he was suffering from concussion. After a fast recovery, the band decided that they would need more security so that nothing like it would happen again. This bad incident, however, did not deter them because they carried on with their only British tour for the album. They played twenty-four shows between October 30th and November 27th.

In December, 1982, a new version of "Hungry Like the Wolf" was released, the Kershenbaum Remix, and it earned the No.3 spot on the charts. After the great success of *Rio*, the world was taken over by what was sometimes called "Fab Five Fever" and "Durandamonium." The band felt like they were on the top of the world.

While Durandamonium occurred, sceptics could never figure out the attraction. The main stereotype was that anyone who was interested in the band were females, on average, between the ages of twelve and nineteen. The principle of aesthetics was thrown into the mix because the sceptics thought these young women were only interested in the band because of their good looks.

While part of that may have been true, there were others who also liked the band for their music and talent. Many of them are still great fans today. Those mostly false claims were easy to make at this time because this was when Duran Duran was reaching the zenith of their career.

If most of these fans were, indeed, teenage girls solely interested in the band's appearance, then some of the sceptics could have been jealous boyfriends who couldn't compare. Nevertheless, it is Duran's Duran's ability to sell music to those who are willing to listen, which allows them to pay their bills.

After the most hectic Christmas that the band had encountered thus far, they decided to settle in New York for a while. This was right before MTV invited them to appear in their second annual New Year's telecast, live from the Savoy Theatre in Manhattan. Although three other bands received the same invitation, Duran Duran had the honour of greeting the east coasters into 1983.

Although things looked promising, the beginning of the year had seen them exhausted and needing a break. 1982 had been a busy and exciting year and they decided to cut their touring schedule back and

Heyday

remain focused on an extensive video project. They wanted to release it without pressure.

They had received many tempting offers by various people for recording projects, but they refused them. The important thing was that they got to relax for the month of January by going home to visit their families and take care of some personal business. John and Andy, who categorise themselves as homebodies, liked the fact that they got to spend time with their loved ones. Going home gave the band members fond memories of the days before their fame.

Shortly after their time off started, workaholic Nick Rhodes found himself bored and looked for other projects on which to embark. It was then that he found an unknown band called Kajagoogoo. Nick saw potential in the band, and he wanted to produce them.

This would be the first of many side projects upon which Nick would embark during his earlier years. Nick co-produced the pop band's debut song, "Too Shy," with Colin Thurston. Some may also claim that "Too Shy" was Kajagoogoo's signature tune — it was certainly the band's most well-known song.

When Nick met the band's lead singer Limahl, his persistence reminded Nick of Duran Duran when they were starting out themselves. He took the tape to EMI and was quite surprised that it reached the No.1 spot on the British charts in February of that year. He also felt confident about the production, and he predicted a lot of fame for Kajagoogoo. While the band had a fair amount of success in the 1980s, they have since faded out of existence for the most part.

In 2004, Kajagoogoo appeared on VH1 for a show called *Bands Reunited*, which reunited broken up eighties' bands for one concert. Kajagoogoo got back together for one performance, but the members of the band didn't get along and stated that this would be the last show they performed together. Other bands, such as Berlin, were featured on the show, and found that their situation was similar to Kajagoogoo's.

On February 9, 1983, Duran Duran saw one of their greatest achievements to date, when they received awards at London's Lyceum for the British Rock and Pop Award ceremony. They won a total of a third of the votes and made their way into the best group category. They had also won the best album award for their second album, *Rio*.

Simon easily won the category of best male singer because over twenty percent of the people voted for him. Unfortunately, the only major category that the band didn't win was the category for best single. The votes were divided between second place for "Save a Prayer" and fourth place for "Hungry Like the Wolf" and "Rio." The fact that the band did well in the other categories marked this as one of the proudest days in their life; they were reaping the rewards of all their hard work. *Rio* remained at the top of the charts for two years, with sales of over five million copies.

Despite the excellent protection the band received when they made public appearances, trouble seemed to have a way of finding them. Duran Duran almost caused a riot on Broadway, and it was not because they were going to perform at the well-known theatre of the same name.

Rather, they were just making their way to the video store. On March 19, 1983, where five thousand teenage fans queued up at the Forty-Ninth Street Video Shack store; the line extended all the way past Forty-Eighth.

All these fans had a reason to be excited because this was the first in-store appearance there for any musical artist. And it just so happened that their favourite band was going to be there to meet and greet their fans. Video Shack worked in conjunction with Capitol Records, and the Sony Consumer Products Company, to make the whole event possible.

The lads were scheduled to make an appearance to promote their reluctantly released video 45. The two songs that it featured were "Hungry Like the Wolf" and "Girls on Film." Of course, many young fans knew about this event because it was heavily broadcast by a local radio station, WPLJ, the previous week. The event was scheduled to start at 2:00 p.m., but the most adamant fans began to show up at 6:00 a.m. Their great dedication had gotten the best of them, and they wanted a chance to see and possibly meet their idols.

Not long after the event was set to start, the members of the band quietly filed in through the back door while being filmed by the Sony video crew. When someone from the crowd spotted them, many of the youth started climbing the gates in front of the store window, and the ones in front were being pushed by the excited fans behind them.

This caused the authorities to panic, so they had to call for extra backup. They were worried that the gates would not hold back the fans who were trying to get through them. Eventually, with the aid of more than 150 police officers, they were able to secure the area. It was during this time that curious onlookers began to observe the area to see what was happening.

After things calmed down, the gates were raised, and the fans began to enter the store in groups of twenty. The anticipation greatly built up, however, and some authorities were afraid that they were going to lose control of the crowd again. The fans who bought the new 45s received autographs, photos, and small greetings from the members of the band.

This was probably considered by many in attendance to be the most exciting day of their lives. After the event was over, Video Shack's director of promotion and advertising reported the events of the day. Close to 200 of the new 45s were sold during the hour and forty-five-minute session.

The sad news for the day came from the results of the ordeal that happened earlier. There were three injuries, including a broken foot. The girl who suffered the broken foot received a phone call from the members of the band a few days later. This was a move of sympathy on Duran Duran's part.

Some hundred fans, who didn't get to go inside the video store during the session, complained to their parents. In turn, the upset parents made phone calls, berating the manager. To appease the fans and their parents, each of those who did not make it in received a complimentary T-shirt, which read, *I was Duran Duraned at Video Shack*. The T-shirts were originally going to be printed for an extra attraction for the next appearance at the store, but the managers made good use of them to cover the situation and to keep themselves out of what could have been another public relations problem.

Even though the event had seen a scary and dangerous beginning, employees at the Video Shack, Capitol Records, and the Sony Corporation were pleased with the overall outcome of the band's promotion. Duran Duran made good sales on their videos, and they got to meet some of the fans who supported them. Being that as it may, all the officials learned a lesson from the potential danger that came so close to rearing its ugly head. They knew from that moment on, they were going to be prepared and exercise any necessary precautions in advance.

In the future, the authorities would be notified ahead of time in case of such an event, which meant that smaller amounts of people, such as groups of ten, would be admitted into the store at one time. They would also enter in a calm and orderly fashion.

The officials also suggested a "calming room," which was to be used as a place where fans could let out their extra energy before going in to meet the band. Fortunately for everyone involved, complete chaos had been avoided, and the event was considered to be a success.

In May 1983, the band decided to relocate to Montserrat. Aside from recording "The Reflex," the five-month experience was not all it was cracked up to be. Part of this was because they weren't impressed with the condition of the recording studio and its equipment.

Nick seemed to suffer the most because being confined to the studio for most of the time took a toll on his health. When he did venture outside he suffered with sunburn as well as a minor case of food poisoning. Nick was worried about the slow progress of the album. What he had was fear of impending doom, medically known as paroxysmal tachycardia. He finally received medical attention, and the doctors told him that the condition was very common and very far from life-threatening.

After the scare, Nick started to take his health more seriously, and he pulled himself together so he could work with the rest of the band on finishing the album.

In July 1983, the band had come close to finishing their third studio album. They had no problems with the rough tapes that were finished, but they felt they needed to get away from the place where they were currently staying.

While the West Indies was nice, it had limited appeal and lacked excitement, according to Nick. The band made many suggestions as to where they could go next, such as Nassau, London, Los Angeles, and New York. But the disadvantages were stronger than the advantages, so they decided to finish the album elsewhere.

Not long after this they decided to go to the other side of the world — Sydney, Australia. The band had not been there since their 1982 *Rio* Tour, which was cut short because of Andy's illness. This was the time that they became a household name. All the members of the band found it a nice area to return to with all the beautiful scenery it had to offer.

*****

Princess Diana was a great fan of Duran Duran in the 1980s; they were her favourite band. She liked them so much that she invited them to perform for husband Prince Charles and herself. The event took place in front of the royal family and forty thousand other fans. The forty-five-minute concert was performed at the Dominion Theatre.

Even though the idea of the performance made them nervous, they never anticipated that anything would really go wrong. Although, as bad luck would have it, things did. John's bass guitar kept going out of tune, and Roger's drum pedal broke. The affect it had on the songs caused them to worry that they would lose favour with the Princess of Wales.

The band performed their final number as they wondered if fate had turned completely against them. To their surprise, they received a standing ovation because many in the audience didn't realise the things that went wrong. They were relieved that they made it through the whole incident virtually unscathed. If anyone noticed what went wrong, no one seemed to care. The "disaster" was either overlooked or forgotten.

Prince Charles and Princess Diana were happy that the band came to perform. The Prince publicly thanked the band for performing before the Royal Family. One could also argue that Duran Duran had received the royal seal of approval given that they were Princess Diana's favourite band.

The band was also known for their benefit and charity shows. Probably one of the most famous examples was their MENCAP concert. MENCAP was an organisation established to aid in the education and treatment for people suffering with a learning disability. They were pleased they had an opportunity to play for such a worthy cause.

The show took place at Aston Villa's ground Villa Park in Birmingham in front of an audience of twenty thousand. Prince Charles opened the event by presenting a speech, after which came performances by The City Beat Band and Robert Palmer. Even though many fans made it a point to sit patiently through the opening speech and performances, they anxiously awaited the main event when Duran Duran took the stage at 8:30 to start their performance.

After the event, even reviewers of the show agreed that the performance was virtually flawless. An observer would not take long to notice the audience had their usual energy, which encouraged the band to do their best. Another thing which excited both the band and their audience was the fact that this was the first live performance of their future hit, "Union of the Snake." They also played their version of Iggy Pop's famous song, "Funtime." The lads were satisfied with the job they had done, and they felt a celebration was in order. The band went to the Rum Runner to unwind after the show.

In order for the band to reach their goals, they had to work hard, which meant putting in eighteen hours a day in the recording studio. On one occasion, the band invited some of their most loyal fans into the EMI Studios to provide background vocals for what was going to be the title track of their new album, *Seven and the Ragged Tiger*.

While the song was, indeed, very catchy, it was eventually scrapped. Another song, called "The Seventh Stranger," was chosen to be placed on the album instead. The eighth track, "Tiger Tiger," was inspired by a poem. Simon was a big admirer of William Blake, the father of English Romanticism. He got the name for the song and other album ideas from one of Blake's most famous poems, "The Tyger."

The first test of the album took place in October when "Union of the Snake" was released worldwide on the 17th of the month. The band was eager to see how fans responded to their new song, and they hoped it would help them achieve just as much success as they had gained in the past. It was released in both "7 and "12 formats. To the band's delight, the song was a phenomenal success, and they received praise for their sophistication and instrumental skill.

Even though the song reached No.3 on the charts in England, the band was disappointed because it had failed to reach No.1. "Union of the Snake," however, earned that spot in the United States, which was a great achievement. The band had already began thinking about tour dates for early 1984 after they learned of their new success.

The video was directed by Simon Milne and included some eye-opening imagery that was inspired by another sci-fi movie, *A Boy and His Dog*. The plot consists of people living in a bleak underground culture, due to nuclear devastation. Simon stumbles onto their "civilisation" and finds that he must escape after their colony is disturbed.

The next thing Duran Duran had to think about how they wanted the new album cover to look. Of course, they wanted to have a tiger in the photograph, but there were no tigers available in Australia. They decided to have the album cover shot on the steps of the State Library of New South Wales.

The whole endeavour, however, turned out to be a long and

Heyday

expensive process because photograph after photograph was rejected. When the band finally decided on one for the cover, the cost was rumoured to have already been over £500,000. Many may have noticed that the photograph of the band and the tiger are on separate parts of the album, which indicates that the shots were taken separately. The animal handlers could not get the tiger's full cooperation.

Since it took longer than planned to complete the album, the band had only ten days to rehearse before their next world tour. The Australian dates were scheduled first. It was then that John and Roger took a promotional trip to Japan. They let people know that they would be back for the eastern part of the *Sing Blue Silver* Tour in the beginning of 1984. This time, everyone participating with the band on tour benefited from their hard work. The first leg of their tour was a great success.

November 21, 1983 saw the release of the third album *Seven and the Ragged Tiger*, which was recorded on the beautiful island of Montserrat in the Caribbean. The significance of the name *Seven and the Ragged Tiger* refers to the five band members and their two managers.

One could get technical and say that this was the last album The Fab Five released, excluding 1984's *Arena*, until 2004. This album produced great singles such as "The Reflex" and "Union of the Snake."

The song "New Moon on Monday" was accompanied by a spectacular video featuring a town similar to that in Nazi Germany during WWII, complete with revolutionaries and fireworks.

The hit single, "Is There Something I Should Know?" was released the same year. After it was added to the band's first album, replacing "To the Shore," *Duran Duran* was re-released, and the album soared to the top of the charts.

The video for "Is There Something I Should Know?" included clips from some of their previous videos, which delighted the millions who watched it on MTV. Since the re-release of their first album included a chart-topping hit, this had a dramatic increase in sales.

By the time the tour reached the United States, fans were most eager for them to return, having not seen the band since they promoted *Rio*. They played to the masses and the shows sold out to thousands of fans. The band knew they had a long tour ahead, but that didn't stop them from going home to visit their loved ones.

Due to their ever-increasing popularity in the States through MTV and extensive radio play, the executives of Capitol Records booked the band to perform on the hugely popular television show *Saturday Night Live*. While this was a good showcase they had to take into consideration the throngs of fans who made it their vocation to follow them everywhere they went. To avoid the impending madness of the crowds, they tried a tactic, which involved repeating announcements of the band's arrival at the JFK airport.

The tactic worked, as it threw off many of the fans. Instead of the large crowds they expected, only a small number of people, a hundred or so, showed up. This hardly attracted enough attention to alert security. Many photographers who anxiously waited to capture the band on film went home disappointed that night. They had only gotten a few candid shots of the band.

During their soundcheck they were heard having fun with playing parodies of popular Rolling Stones and Billy Joel songs. The band was so raucous during this mock rehearsal that a stagehand, who was growing impatient with their antics, told them to stop.

Later tales of their boredom soon came into play. When the band relied on their odd sense of humour in such times. Simon is known for his prankish humour, and he decided one night that it would be fun to play a little prank on his friends. He showed up for a soundcheck with his arm in a sling and told the other members of the band that he slipped on some ice outside.

After hearing this, the rest of the band wanted to cancel the show, but they decided to go through with it. Members of the crew rushed to accompany Simon by rearranging things to his comfort. Nearly two hours later, Andy unknowingly approached Simon and asked him how he was going to clap his hands to get the audience started for the songs.

The enthusiastic singer replied, "Like this!" as he lifted up his hands and threw off the sling. While Andy and the others were relieved to know that Simon was all right, they didn't know whether to laugh at his antic or be angry with him.

Their performance on *Saturday Night Live*, was a wonderful showcase and the fans who had chosen that night to go to the studio were glad they did.

After the show, although tired they autographed hundreds of photos; they also patiently posed for new ones. The night was filled with pandemonium as they interacted with their fans. While the band enjoyed the attention and excitement of it all, they found certain things to be annoying. Nick stated one of his pet peeves was fans trying to rip off the sleeves and buttons of hard-to-replace clothes.

Although he didn't like this, he sympathised with the actions of the fans. He remembered being a fan of someone himself. Every time Nick saw a kid standing outside waiting for tickets, he was reminded of the time he did the same thing when he was a young fan of Bryan Ferry.

Both the band and the fans were expecting the great success they received from *Rio* and the tours surrounding. At the time they started their *Sing Blue Silver* Tour, they stepped off a plane at the Kennedy Airport. This seemed to parallel the incident with The Beatles in 1964. Some of the band members shrugged it off, but this was the year that they were going to conquer the world. While this incident was nowhere near as dangerous, it was reminiscent of what happened at the Video Shack where a large number of fans had come out to support them as they arrived.

During this time, Simon got engaged to his girlfriend, Claire Stansfield, a model from Canada. Claire was born in England and moved to Canada with her family at a young age. She started modelling during her early teens, but she didn't feel it was her true calling. She then switched careers and began acting, which became her main focus for the rest of her life. Her meeting with Simon was one of circumstance, and it was rather unusual.

Although Claire was not a big fan of Duran Duran, she went to see them in her hometown of Toronto. Claire spent most of the night at a bar talking with her friends, but they went to another bar after the show and ran into the band. When she met Simon, she asked him what he did. Claire was probably one of the few people at the time who did not recognise him. From the moment they met, he had fallen head over heels for her. Simon instantly invited her to a party, but she cautiously turned him down because they'd just met.

Not to be deterred, Simon phoned Claire from every city where he toured and finally convinced her to go out with him. The couple began dating, but they never spent much time together until they met in Montserrat.

At first, Claire had to bide her time sunbathing, while Simon spent many long hours in the studio. Once they finally could spend some real time together, Claire decided she was ready to be put to the ultimate test, to face the approval or disapproval of the fans. Luckily, most had grown fond of Claire and treated her with kindness and respect. Although, many were jealous that she had Simon's affection.

There are always some, however, who had the idea that as each of the band members decided to marry, Duran Duran's popularity would start to decrease. Upon hearing this, the band members decided that they wouldn't let such a trivial thing interfere with their music-making career. Some of them made the claim that marriage would provide them with the stability they would need to last them through their lives and career. They were not worried about these alleged "adverse effects" because they knew their truest fans would remain loyal.

In November 1983, they began their world tour of Australia, and five of their biggest shows were performed at Wembley Arena. The tour promised great success. And as a result, they scheduled some shows in the United States. This was a pivotal turning point, selling out a record number of shows. The success that their new album and tour had reached was the band's biggest to date.

The dates spilled into 1984, and while the band was in the United States, they received two Grammy awards. One was for a compilation video that contained their first eleven videos, and the other was for song clips of "Hungry Like the Wolf." They beat Michael Jackson in this category. By 1984, Duran Duran's biggest feat of playing to a sold-out crowd was accomplished. In February of the same year, they posed for their famous cover photo in *Rolling Stone* Magazine.

During the summer of 1984, Roger Taylor married his love, Giovanna Cantone. The ceremony was held in Naples, Italy, in a church called the Capo Di Monte. They chose that location for the benefit of all the distant relatives, who found they could not attend a wedding in England. Roger and Giovanna met in Birmingham, where they both grew up.

Simon was the best man at the ceremony, and a close friend of Giovanna's was the maid of honour. Unfortunately, Andy and Tracey could not make it to the wedding because she was expecting their first child. The birth had gone well, but Tracey suffered severe depression and mood swings for weeks after their son was born.

The words of the ceremony were recited in both English and Italian. While the ceremony was happening, various members of the press waited outside the church doors to get word on what was going on inside.

A romantic touch which was added to the ceremony consisted of

Roger and Giovanna kissing each other's rings before placing them on each other's fingers. The mood took the entire crowd by storm, as it invoked tears of joy. Simon's attendance was on the back of numerous rumours of his separation with Claire. Giovanna's gown was designed by the famous David Emanuel, whose creations were worn by many celebrities, including Princess Diana.

The reception was held on a boat, which set sail around the island of Capri. This created a romantic mood for the newly appointed bride and groom. Entertainment for everyone included live music and fireworks going off in the night-time sky. Roger and Giovanna's honeymoon consisted of a cruise up the Nile.

Love was also in the air for Nick who married on August 1, 1984 at a London Registrar's office to his model girlfriend, Julie Anne Friedman, an Iowa heiress. The couple met at a party in 1982.

Two weeks later, she told her mother and father she was going to go on tour with the band. Her parents, Bill and Jo Anne Freidman, were pillars of the Des Moines community. Bill was president of Yonkers, a chain of twenty-nine Midwest retail stores. Being that the Friedmans had old-fashioned values, they were all but pleased to find this out. They didn't think the situation was appropriate or wholesome. Bill and Jo Anne were showing their parental concern for Julie Anne, but she didn't choose to heed their warning.

The Friedmans, however, began to warm up to Nick after they met him on August 1st, 1983, in New York. They made the assertion that he treated their daughter very well, which was most important to them. They were fond of the fact that Nick and Julie Anne shared the same interest and love for certain things, such as art deco and fine wine.

The wedding consisted of an unusual pink ensemble, including six live pink flamingos. Julie Anne was dressed in a tight pink and white gown, while Nick wore a pale blue shirt and a mauve cutaway with tails. Nick was said to have worn almost as much makeup, if not more, than Julie Anne. Whatever rumours Duranies may have heard about the best man being a woman were true. The role was taken by singer Elayne Griffiths, who was Nick's best friend (and ex-girlfriend).

Aside from the other members of Duran Duran, only immediate family were invited to attend since the ceremony was small. This also included royal photographer, Norman Parkinson, who was there to shoot photos which, allegedly, were not to be shown on MTV.

At least 400 devotees of the band waited outside the hotel as the guests arrived for the dinner, which consisted of salmon and stuffed lamb. Even more excitement occurred when Simon arrived with Claire, and he hinted that he may be the next member of the band to marry.

The wedding cake was a three-tiered cake from Harrods. The reception was long, and the dancing continued until 1:00 a.m., where, immediately, after the couple returned to their parents so they could open the gifts they received. The Friedman's gave them a sterling silver set made to serve twelve. Although the wedding was unorthodox, Julie Anne's parents were relieved to know that their daughter was happy and that their union was legitimised.

Nick's parents were shocked by the news and nowhere near as enthusiastic about the affair as suspected. While Roger and Sylvia Bates claimed that they did not dislike the bride to be, they felt that Nick was too young for marriage. When they were asked about this on the wedding day, his father stated that he would rather not respond to the question.

The Freidmans, however, took control of the event and celebrated with the seventy-five guests from their side. The guests spent their nights in expensive suites at the Savoy, from where they had organised parties, which included a cruise down the River Thames.

The next day, the new couple left for their honeymoon, consisting of a three-week cruise on a private yacht to the Greek Islands. The Friedmans never admitted how much the whole affair cost, but they felt that their daughter's happiness and the prosperity of Nick joining the family made it all worth the expense.

John was dating his girlfriend, Janine Andrews, at the time. She was a former Bond girl who had a role as a female cult member in the movie *Octopussy*. The couple was known for having a stormy relationship, and they began to experience some turbulence when she said that she didn't want to get married as John would have liked to do.

Janine was quoted, many times, as stating that she did not want to settle down. The thought of a homebody lifestyle and spending the rest of her days with only one man, for the most part, nauseated her.

While Janine also stated that she was monogamous to John, she didn't want the pressures that came along with marriage. Many fans didn't quite know what to make of the news, especially since they didn't know if Janine's claims of being monogamous were true. Whether fans wanted the relationship to thrive or fall apart, they were all anxious to find out what was going to happen. It wasn't much longer, however, when John and Janine broke up because of their differences.

Many Duranies knew that Nick has always taken his music seriously, but some were surprised to find that he had further extended his talents by taking up photography. Nick also gained acclaim with the release of his photography book, *Interference*, which consists of Polaroid pictures taken of television screens on which various images were distorted. *Interference* was well-received, and Nick's fans were eager to purchase his new work. Nick always had a great interest in photography, and he thought of this as a great opportunity to express himself.

The band's career was in high gear, and their live album, *Arena*, was compiled with songs recorded from their tour around the world. The following year, the hour-long video with the same title was released with most of the same songs from the record.

Russell Mulcahy directed the movie and incorporated his ideas into the film. He used his creative license by thinking of great ideas for *Arena*. The video is complete with Duran Duran performing a concert in L.A. and their antagonist, Durand Durand, again played by Milo O' Shea, suffered delusions of grandeur. He wanted all the innocent concertgoers to know that he was "the real Duran Duran." The rest of the movie consisted of the evil astronaut taking away various members of the audience while the band played on, unaware. *Arena* also contained a few clips from the movie *Barbarella*.

It was the same kind of concept as the sci-fi flick, but the good Duran Duran actually defeated the evil Durand Durand. The video was choreographed by Arlene Phillips, whose dancers performed violent moves that fit well with the situation of the film. While some found that they could not decipher the meaning of the movie at first, they later felt free to interpret it. The second part of the title clarified that the whole concept, indeed, was considered "an absurd notion."

Their hit single, "The Wild Boys," reached No.4 on the U.S. charts. The song was included in *Arena* and played as a separate video on MTV. "The Wild Boys" received its name from the title of a book written by William S. Burroughs. There are many different parts of the book, and the one that was actually called "The Wild Boys" presented characters, which served as inspiration to the band.

Duran Duran also had the screen rights to Burroughs's novel. All in all, the book is homosexual fantasy about these wild boys who create new men via artificial insemination, men who have never even

Reach Up For The Sunrise

seen or knew about women. This allowed them to base the characters on the novel. "The Wild Boys" was produced by Nile Rodgers.

As some may remember, Simon encountered some problems while he was filming the video. During the scene in which he was strapped to the moving windmill, he was singing the lyrics of the song. At one point, the windmill stopped with Simon's head still underwater. It was nearly a minute before it started working again, and Simon came up for air.

He recalled many people made a bigger deal of the incident than it really was, but he also admitted that he was a bit frightened while the whole thing was going on.

The song used in the video was actually the extended mix of "The Wild Boys," also known as the "Wilder Than Wild Boys" Extended Mix. A censored and shortened video that matched the duration of the regular song was made to run on MTV. This video was very high budget. In fact, it had the largest budget to date, which is really quite amazing.

"The Wilder Than Wild Boys" Extended Mix is included on the 1999 album, *Strange Behaviour*. This compilation includes hits from their first self-titled album (*Duran Duran*) to their second (*The Wedding Album*).

Shortly after finishing their 1984 North American tour, a documentary video was released. The video is called *Sing Blue Silver*, and it includes various footage taken as they went on tour from city to city. The tour started in Calgary, Alberta, Canada on January 30, and it ended nearly three months later in San Francisco, California on April 17. During that time, the band played many shows and reached a total audience of 543,000 fans.

Some of the most memorable things that took place in the video consisted of shots of random excitement from the fans at the beginning of one of the shows. One could easily view this chaos as a typical day in the early life of Duran Duran while they were being followed on tour. There was also a lot of commentary from the tour's production manager, Spy Matthews, as he tried to make sure all operations were running smoothly.

The lads also got to share their moment in the spotlight with a few others. Backstage, before one of their shows, they got to meet two members of the L.A. Raiders, Mike Davis and Marcus Allen. The Raiders were the 1984 Super Bowl champions. The band was presented with personalised football jerseys, with the team colours and their names on the back.

Sing Blue Silver came out toward the end of 1984 on VHS and laserdisc. It was released on DVD in April 2004. Included are many things which may not have been known to most fans until its release. Simon and Nick talked about image recording.

One of the things they emphasised included the importance of self-confidence while thinking of ways on how to be remembered. Roger contributed to the discussion by making the statement that Duran Duran wanted to be remembered for their musical talent as well as their great videos.

One of the most comical and memorable moments featured in the video was when John told the tour sponsors from Coca-Cola that he preferred Pepsi after one spokesperson made a slightly condescending remark toward him. Another such moment included footage of Simon's aforementioned prank, which consisted of him clapping after he fooled his bandmates into thinking that he had injured his arm.

The last portion of *Sing Blue Silver*, before the credits, showed the boys in a fond embrace after they performed their final show in San Francisco. Even though their tour was successful, they questioned what they were going to do once it ended.

Through its good use of information spanning the duration of the tour, those watching the video or DVD got to see pieces of Duran Duran on their most successful tour to date. Some of the songs featured in *Sing Blue Silver* include "Hungry Like the Wolf," "Careless Memories," "Planet Earth," "Rio," "Is There Something I Should Know," "The Wild Boys," "Girls on Film," and "Tiger Tiger."

During Christmas 1984, the band became part of the great charity project *Band Aid*. Many of the UK's most famous musicians, such as Phil Collins and Paul McCartney, got together to record "Do They Know It's Christmas?" All proceeds from the benefit went to try to relieve people in Ethiopia from starvation and other dire conditions that existed over there.

The original Band Aid recording was what inspired the American equivalent, "We Are the World," only a few months later. The organisation was founded in 1984, by Bob Geldof of the Irish band Boomtown Rats and Midge Ure from Ultravox.

Some may also remember Geldof as Pink, the lead character in the 1982 film version of Pink Floyd's *The Wall*. John would have also made a good Pink, if he was a little older at the time, because he resembled Bob Geldof.

The recording studio was loaned to the founders of the event and the performers for twenty-four hours on November 25, 1984. The main recording of the songs took place from 11:00 a.m. to 7:00 p.m. until they were satisfied with their work on the song.

The record was promoted by Bob Geldof the following morning, but he ran into problems with the British government because they were not going to let all the money be donated to the charity. The government refused to wave the taxes for the single sales. It was not until Bob stood up to Prime Minister Margaret Thatcher that the government was convinced to give the tax money back to the charity.

When the record was released on December 15, it became a phenomenal success and soared to No.1. "Do They Know It's Christmas?" remained at the same position for five weeks, selling over three million copies, making it the best-selling single in the UK at that time.

The name Band Aid had a double meaning. It not only meant providing assistance to the nations in need, but it also symbolised healing the world. Band Aid was reformed three times because Midge Ure believed that every generation should have its own version.

Elsewhere board games seemed to be popular in the 1980s. People played them just as regularly as they go online today and play games in cyberspace. While no one has the chance to log onto any official website and have one of the band members play the part of an entrepreneur, one can always bring him or herself back to real life. He or she can relive the joys of the board game that was created for the band.

The game to which I refer is called *Duran Duran: Into the Arena*, which was produced by Milton Bradley in 1985. The main premise involves collecting chips that list popular song titles from the band. The game looked simple enough, but the directions presented on the sheet were anything but for new players to figure out. Even though this was the case, the game is considered a collector's item by many Duranies.

The band was now at the height of their fame. The *Sing Blue Silver* Tour proved to be a great success, and the boys had the world at their beckon call. After having completed all this, however, they needed time to slow things down and allow themselves to unwind.

Even though the band was taking a break from all major projects, John had the urge to keep going. He has always been one to keep his eye on things, especially things that caught his interest. He found out that the new James Bond movie, *A View to a Kill*, was in the beginning stages of production. The fact that he happens to be a big 007 fan made him decide to try and further extend his talents so that he could get on the movie soundtrack.

John approached the movie's producer, Cubby Broccoli, and told him that he thought the movie should have a good song to match the theme. John truly believed that Duran Duran could produce this great song to help advertise the movie. Needless to say, the band got the job, so they set themselves to work on the track.

"A View to a Kill" was released as a single in May, while the movie came out in theatres on Christmas 1985. They did a great job on the song, and it gave them much acclaim to match their hard work. 1985 seemed to be their best year to date because they were at the height of their career, and they had numerous accomplishments behind them. However, there were still many rumours about the band breaking up, which dismayed their fans, many of whom remained in denial of the possibly that this could happen.

Reach Up For The Sunrise

CHAPTER 4

Times in the Life of Simon Le Bon

Simon always had a passion for sailing, so he, along with the Berrow brothers, commissioned Skip Novak to build the Drum. It was a large sailboat which was entered in the 605-mile Fastnet yacht race. Simon had hopes that this race would prepare him for the 1985 Whitbread Round the World Race. The vessel ended up costing £1.6 million to build.

While everyone involved anticipated a smooth race, the Drum gave the crew trouble no more than six hours into the race. One of the bearings dropped off. As a result, the entire steering system was rendered unsupported, and the problem took nearly three hours to fix.

Of course, no one was quite aware of the danger that this occurrence would later pose to the crew. The weather conditions were ominous once the boat rounded Dodman Point. By the time the Drum reached the Cornish village of Portscatho, the fourteen-foot keel snapped off and caused the boat to overturn. Simon and four others were trapped when the water pressure captured them under the hull. They were there for nearly twenty minutes, with only a small pocket of air to keep them alive.

Although the ordeal was over, most of the information was not relayed to the public until Simon told his story. Two days later, Simon talked to Laura Sanderson, a *People* Magazine correspondent. Simon started by providing the information that he was just finished with a four-hour watch working the main sheet.

He retreated below the deck and was just on the verge of falling asleep when the boat turned over. Both he and Rick, who was one of his partners in the race, were thrown out of their bunks. It did not take long for them to realise the danger they all were in. Rick and Simon moved toward the hatch as they tried to escape; they were afraid that the two heavy sails would fall on them.

They scrambled right before the whole boat turned over and they became trapped underneath it. The men, however, did their best not to panic because they knew that it would get them nowhere. If they wanted to get themselves out of this situation, the crew would have to remain calm.

Three minutes after the Drum flipped over, there was a new ray of hope, as an automatic radio beacon signal was activated by seawater. The yacht Carat was directly behind the Drum when they noticed that the boat lost its rigging because it could no longer be seen on the horizon. They didn't take another moment to hesitate investigating what happened.

As the small crew waited to be rescued, they had gotten a hold of some lifesavers. While Simon knew that he should not panic, he was greatly concerned because his youngest brother Johnny was also on the boat. As soon as the rescue crew arrived, they took nearly five minutes to rescue Simon, and he almost died.

When Larry Slater, a petty officer and trained diver, came to rescue Simon, he was working with a member of the crew, Terry Gould. Larry went from the helicopter into the water and he guided Terry to the rest of the crewmembers, who were still trapped underneath the boat.

As soon as Larry Slater reached Simon, he gave him a life jacket with a breathing tube, but Simon had to let go of the object because it increased his buoyancy. Simon took a deep breath and completed the most difficult part of the task, which consisted of making his way up to the surface.

He had to fight through all the ropes that hung down from the deck that could have very easily gotten tangled in, which would have made his chances for survival very slim. When Simon got free, water went up his nose, and he found that he started breathing too early as he was still underwater.

After Simon and the other crewmembers were rescued, they were dropped off in a cow field in the village of Portscatho. The first substance that Simon encountered on land was dung from one of the cows. As disgusting as that sounds, Simon didn't care that he happened to set his foot down in the substance because he was happy and greatly relieved to be alive.

Shortly after, they were dropped off at a farmhouse, where they were wrapped in blankets to keep them warm. Their hosts also provided them with tea to help warm their insides. Although, in the heat of the moment, they portrayed shock and horror, they were all glad they hadn't lost their lives. The nearly tragic incident made the boat the cover of *People* on August 26, 1985.

Simon said that millions of thoughts crossed his mind. He thought that he was never going to see his family or his new girlfriend, Yasmin, again. Some could say that the incident changed his life because it was a "wakeup call." Simon felt that it was time for him to settle down and start a family of his own. This was something that he never seriously considered before.

While everyone was alive and safe, Simon found himself concerned with the insurance of the Drum. He and his partners still oversaw the salvage operation. The final amount was enormous with towing and repairs, which added up to a total cost of over £400,000. Although the task was going to be difficult, costly, and time-consuming, the crew wanted to have the boat fully restored.

As for the mystery of the Fastnet mishap, it remained just that, a mystery. A week after the incident, the boat's designer, Ron Holland, flew in from Ireland so that he could inspect the remains. Ron soon found that he was perplexed by the whole thing, saying that it was a freak accident.

Then the crew's captain, Skip Novak, said the accident was due to a structural flaw, hinting that the vessel should have been durable enough to face any challenge. Skip met Simon at the Swan World Cup in Sardinia in the autumn of 1984. It seemed that the designer was not prepared to accept responsibility for what happened.

Simon's mother stated that he always divided his love for sailing and music equally, and when he began to express his love for sailing, Ann grew concerned. She made the statement that she and Simon's father braced themselves for this sort of danger. John, however, stated that he was mainly concerned with the fact that his sons looked out for each other. The Le Bons trusted their sons and knew that they would keep one another in check, but there was still a lot of room for parental concern.

While Ann and John were at home watching television, they received an anonymous phone call, telling them about the bad news concerning the Drum accident. Although Ann was informed that everyone was all right, she never got a chance to find out who made the call because the person hung up after delivering the news.

Hours later, the Le Bons got another phone call informing them that both the boys were safe. Since Simon and John were separated during the accident, neither knew if the other survived. According to Ann, the brothers had always been very close, and not knowing how the other was at the time caused them both mental anguish. Andy blamed the Drum accident on the Berrow brothers.

The whole ordeal was a traumatic event for Simon's new model girlfriend, Yasmin Parvanah. She had joined her parents in Cowes on the Isle of Wight to wish her boyfriend bon voyage. Yasmin's mother, Patricia, said she was very concerned when she found out that there were some people trapped inside the hull, but she knew that Simon's bravery and perseverance would see him through.

On the night of the twenty-four-crew rescue, the members were joined by their wives and girlfriends. Yasmin drove for six hours without stopping. She took only a minute to pack a few essential items in a bag before driving off to meet him. Although what happened was nearly tragic, those who arrived in Falmouth found the mood to be uplifting.

The party in the bar of the hotel lasted until 4:00 a.m. Simon was so glad to be reunited with Yasmin that he held her hand all night, and they frequently kissed. One could easily detect the amount of affection they had for each other. The incident was over, and his life was starting to return to normal, par the life of an international pop star.

Despite the fact that others tried to persuade him in the other direction, Simon was determined to go ahead with the race. Nearly two months later, on September 28, 1985, the Drum set sail again from Portsmouth to be included in the Whitbread Round-the-World Race. It came in third place, which inspired Simon to write the song "Grey Lady of the Sea." Although Simon was not on board for this race, he made plans to compete again once he finished more work.

On December 27, 1985, Simon married Yasmin. This left John the last single member of the band. When Simon met Yasmin in 1984, he was still engaged to Claire. He continued to date both Claire and Yasmin at the same time, but the engagement was broken not long after that.

While the breakup was emotional and stressful, Simon and Claire decided to remain friends. Claire moved on and started to branch out more in her career. It wasn't much later when she began to date singer David Austin. She also went on to star in various movies and television shows and made guest appearances on *Xena: Warrior Princess*.

Claire also had parts in the *X-Files* series, *Frasier* (1994) and a small part in Oliver Stone's 1991 movie, *The Doors*. She resides in Los Angeles today. Her work is well-known in the science fiction and the fantasy genre, as she was nicknamed the "sci-fi queen" by her co-workers and fans. Claire married her current husband in 2004.

Despite their lavish lifestyle, Simon and Yasmin wanted to have a simple wedding, both claiming that extravagant ceremonies made too public were annoying. The wedding took place in Yasmin's hometown of Oxford, and the ceremony lasted for fifteen minutes with a total of approximately forty guests. Although the wedding was small and simple, it was enough for the couple to prove their eternal love to one another.

The reception immediately following the ceremony was also small. It was considered more of a party than a reception because of the small number of the guests who were in attendance. The party consisted of the guests, who were staying at a hotel nearby. They feasted on salmon and roast lamb while drinking Champagne. The newlyweds celebrated their honeymoon in Scotland and the south of France.

Yasmin was born on October 29, 1964. She is half English (on her mother's side) and half Iranian (on her father's side). When she was seventeen, she was spotted and recruited by a model agency scout, and she began her career as a model. Nearly two years later, Simon discovered her while flipping through pictures in a magazine when he came across her picture in which she modelled for an advert.

Simon liked what he saw, so he decided to contact the agency to get her information and give her a call. He invited her to the movie premiere of *Indiana Jones and the Temple of Doom*. Yasmin thought that he was playing a joke on her, so she didn't accept his invitation. Her reply was something along the lines of she would rather go out on a date with Rod Stewart.

Simon kept persisting until he convinced her to go out with him. As was the case with his relationship with Claire, things started off a bit slow before for the romance fully escalated.

Things got serious in Paris during the spring of 1985, when the two really started to fall for each other. Months later, Simon knew it felt right with Yasmin, he decided it was time to make his move. They took their wedding vows and happily settled into their first five months of matrimony.

In 1986, Yasmin suffered a miscarriage. The couple was deeply saddened by their loss, and they maintained that they didn't want to try to have another child for a few more years. They admitted they wanted to spend more time together, as a couple, before they tried again to start a family. They also knew they still had plenty of time to have children.

Simon and Yasmin are still happily married, and they have three children, together: Amber Rose Tamara, Saffron Sahara, and Tallulah Pine. The couple celebrated their 35th wedding anniversary on December 27, 2020.

CHAPTER 5

The Breakup

The year was 1985, a year which many rue as the breakup of The Fab Five. Roger was the first to leave — he claimed that he'd had his fill of the band's glamorous lifestyle and that he wanted some privacy.

Rumours followed, and Roger was hounded by the press, who asked why he decided to leave. During one particular incident Roger recalled hearing a knock at his door. He decided to answer it, despite what he had on at the time: A few days of stubble on his face and his wife's pink nightgown. He was surprised to find various members of the press, who took numerous photos of him, at the same time asking him about his departure.

Since Roger was shy; he didn't like doing interviews, especially after having left the band. He preferred the time he spent on the farm with his family.

There was also another instance where Roger and John met for drinks when John tried to convince him to re-join the band. He apologetically declined the offer however, because he liked his life the way it was.

Despite the fact that Roger prefers the quiet life, he also claims to have wanderlust because he feels the need to constantly be moving. If he is one place for too long a time, he has the urge to uproot and move on.

Soon after Roger left, Andy followed. Initially, Andy wanted to take six months off because he got frustrated with the constant demand for creating more hits, and all the stress caused him to burn out.

The breakup saw the band moving in two different directions. Even though these "side projects" started to become established before Duran Duran officially broke up, I felt that they would best be explained after the fact.

Reach Up For The Sunrise

Probably the more famous of the two 1985 side projects was The Power Station. The group was formed by singer Robert Palmer ("Addicted to Love"), Tony Thompson, (drummer for Chic), Andy and John Taylor. The group released their first record, *The Power Station*, in 1985. Hits from the album included "Some Like It Hot" and a cover version of the 1971 T-Rex hit "Get It On."

Originally Bebe Buell (former Playboy model), a short-time girlfriend of John's, was going to provide vocals, but the two of them broke up shortly after John read a tabloid press article about all the musicians she had dated before (including his idol, Steven Tyler, with whom she had a daughter, actress Liv Tyler).

The cover of the song was then put on hold for a few years until The Power Station with Robert Palmer on vocals. The band received a great amount of publicity when they appeared on the popular television show *Miami Vice*, which was something Andy wanted to do.

The band recorded a song especially for their appearance on the show. "We Fight for Love" was featured on the episode and the *Miami Vice II* soundtrack. Andy played guitar and provided vocals for the song. The title was originally going to be "Somewhere, Someone, Somehow," but it was promptly renamed.

John met Robert Palmer in 1982, and John had it in his mind that he wanted to work with Robert on a project. The two of them talked about collaborating during the MENCAP concert in 1983. As more time passed, John recruited Andy, who was more than eager to embark on the project. Mick Jagger and David Bowie were also under consideration to be included somehow.

As soon as the Taylors heard Robert's voice with the recorded tracks, "Get It On," and "Some Like It Hot," they decided that Mick Jagger and David Bowie wouldn't fit into the project. John made demo tapes full of songs and sent them to Robert. He was anxious to get feedback, and, luckily, Robert didn't hold John's pop image against him. He also thought that the tapes showed promising characteristics. Not long after that, they got together with Tony Thompson and formed what they were proud to call The Power Station.

John enjoyed the project and took his new work very seriously. The Power Station liked what they were doing, and their new work proved to be successful. John found he was comfortable after working with Robert and Tony for only a short time. He felt like they had been working together for years.

The Breakup

Robert Palmer admitted that he wasn't much of a fan of Duran Duran's music because he found a lot of it to be too commercial, but he embraced the idea of a side project he found desirable.

Palmer recalled the fun he had producing The Power Station's first album, commonly known as *33⅓*, and he liked the great enthusiasm with which it was produced. However he decided not to tour with The Power Station as he didn't want the commercial fame that Duran Duran usually received.

Robert stayed behind to finish his solo record, while the band began to tour. This left the position open for a suitable replacement singer. Soon after, Michael Des Barres, who had been in the seventies Glam Rock band Silverhead (and whose former wife is the famous groupie Pamela Des Barres) came on board. Des Barres has been a musician since the age of fourteen. Although he produced five albums, he had little performing credit to his name. Des Barres was more than glad to jump at the invitation to join the band. He fit well with The Power Station and provided his skills as a great vocalist, which saw them through their tour.

John made it no secret that he was pleased with the calibre of the music The Power Station made, but there were many rumours that he also wanted to go back and make pop music. John wanted some of their sound to be similar to Duran Duran. Some even made the claim that John got depressed over the whole situation, and he wished that he was working with Duran Duran again. John however, enjoyed his work with The Power Station, despite what others had said.

The Power Station made their debut in 1985 on *Saturday Night Live*. Their hit single, "Some Like It Hot," was at No.14 on the British charts at the time. By May the single made it to No.6 in the States. Two months later, the phenomenal cover of the T-Rex hit, "Get It On," hit the charts, and gained popularity in both England and the States. Andy recalled just how crazy a time it was because the movie *Arena* came out around the same time as The Power Station's debut album.

This was before Duran Duran announced their breakup, and things had moved faster than ever. Andy also recalled all the partying they had done and the money that was spent on such a hedonistic lifestyle. Despite all the fun they had and the success they achieved as a side project to Duran Duran, fans felt that there was something missing. Many, however, were not fond of the fact that Robert Palmer left the band.

Reach Up For The Sunrise

****

Following Band Aid, two concerts took place on July 13, 1985 at Wembley Stadium in London and at the J.F.K. Stadium in Philadelphia under the guise of Live Aid.

Amongst the artists who performed at the American venue were; Madonna, a reformed Led Zeppelin (with Tony Thompson and Phil Collins on drums), Tina Turner and Bob Dylan (with Ronnie Wood, and Keith Richards).

The show lasted fourteen hours, with The Power Station and Duran Duran both performing and Duran Duran as one of the main attractions.

The Power Station was announced around 6:45 p.m. Their brief, but outstanding performance comprised of their hit songs "Murderess" and "Bang a Gong (Get It On)." The song was originally just called "Get It On," but it was renamed in the United States to avoid confusion between that one and the one by Chase. This was the band's first international appearance with their new singer, Michael Des Barres.

Chevy Chase introduced Duran Duran approximately two hours later. The band started with their new hit from the James Bond movie, *A View to a Kill*. The song with the same title as the movie, made its way to No.1 on the charts the very same day. Other songs Duran Duran performed included "The Reflex," "Union of the Snake," and "Save a Prayer." The audience was — needless to say — very enthusiastic to see the band perform live again.

The concert ended with a grand finale after 11:00 p.m., which included a performance of the song "We Are the World," a number for which all the stars had gathered together to sing. The Live Aid performances were a phenomenal success raising over seventy million dollars for its cause.

The band stayed at the Philadelphia Palace, which was reserved at the time for the musicians who performed at the concert. Security was heightened in case there were too many people who tried to get too close to any of the performers. Unbeknownst to most fans, however, this would be the last time The Fab Five line-up would perform onstage until the early 2000s.

****

The Breakup

Meanwhile, there was also word that Simon and Nick were tired of having nothing to do with their spare time. They decided to have a side project of their own. Nick Rhodes was anxious to get started. Simon had just gotten back from his vacation, and he received a phone call from Nick saying that he wanted to make an album of their own. Simon agreed to produce the album, but his enthusiasm, at first, left much to be desired. Arcadia was formed, and their first and only album, *So Red the Rose*, was recorded in France. Their popularity started to rise later in the year.

Like The Power Station, Arcadia also shot videos for their songs, the most memorable of them being, "Election Day." The song climbed to the top 10 on the charts in both the United States and England. The band consisted of Simon, Nick, and Roger. Roger, however, was rarely seen in any of the band photos or videos.

Although their videos contained great elements of creativity, they did not compare to the Duran Duran classics such as "Rio" and "Hungry Like the Wolf."

Probably one of the most interesting videos that the band made was "The Flame," which is loosely based on the movie *The Rocky Horror Picture Show*, and features Simon dressed up as a character resembling Brad Majors, played by Barry Bostwick in the film.

"Say the Word" was another single produced by the band, but it didn't make the album. The song was made for the *Playing for Keeps* movie soundtrack in 1985.

Even though he was not in the forefront, Roger said that he enjoyed being a part of Arcadia. It was a time in his life when he was really satisfied with his music. This helped him enter the recording studio with an open mind, not knowing the final product and sound of the album.

Other people who contributed to the band consisted of talented personnel, such as Herbie Hancock and Grace Jones. The latter of the two provided the spoken parts in the song "Election Day." Arcadia differed from The Power Station's rock 'n' roll sound. Its soothing melodies and thought-provoking lyrics proved the fact that the album had substance.

Although *So Red the Rose* saw some success, not as many fans seemed to appreciate the different style of music portrayed on the album. In fact, some find it hard to categorise Arcadia's music as it was inspired by many different categories. These include pop and

Reach Up For The Sunrise

what Nick has referred to as "gypsy folk." Those who were curious about the term "gypsy folk" soon encountered an example of it. I like to refer to it as "progressive pop."

Shortly after *So Red the Rose* was released, fans of both Duran Duran and Arcadia were asking if either band had plans to tour. As it turned out Arcadia didn't tour to promote their album. They did, however, have an opportunity to work with other talented musicians, such as Pat Metheny, who played bass guitar for the songs. Mark Egan played and arranged the sounds.

Japanese guitarist, Masami, provided some of the more interesting sounds on the album, which gave it an Eastern feel. David Van Tieghem and Rafael De Jesus, both of Talking Heads, played percussion. Andy Mackay of Roxy Music played sax. Other famous artists who worked with Arcadia include Pink Floyd's David Gilmour, Steve Jordan, (who provided drums) and Sting. While the band may have been disappointed that they didn't tour, they had an impressive list of people with whom they worked.

Arcadia found this challenging and rewarding in itself, no matter their genre of music. "Election Day" was released in October 1985. The song made the top twenty in the United States and earned No.7 on the UK charts. With Grace Jones doing a monologue and Andy Mackay playing saxophone, "Election Day" was a song that contained unique and interesting elements. The whole idea behind the message was that people should make decisions knowing that something ground-breaking was going to happen.

Nick emphasised that freedom was the key element that made the song work. *So Red the Rose* had a worldwide release in November. While it managed to make No.23 on the charts in the United States, it had to settle for seven spots lower at No.30 in the UK.

Since Roger was in both The Power Station and Arcadia, he did have to divide his loyalty between the two bands. He was not greatly involved in either project and he began to withdraw himself from both, just as he had with Duran Duran. Too many years in the limelight caused him great stress and nearly led him to have a nervous breakdown.

Also in October, the fourth song off the album, "Communication," would prove to be The Power Station's last single. It was written by Robert Palmer, describing his collaborative relationship with John Taylor. While the song made the top 40 in the States, the band was disappointed it didn't do better. It seemed that many of the fans were

The Breakup

forgetting about The Power Station and the hits that they produced. By that time, the song "Communication" sank to No.75 on the UK charts; the band's fame had more or less ended.

While both these groups had their own following, neither one of them generated the success that Duran Duran had known thus far.

Reach Up For The Sunrise

CHAPTER 6

Moving Along

November 1986 saw the release of Duran Duran's fourth album *Notorious*. The album was produced by Nile Rodgers, formerly of Chic. He was known for his funk music, and he provided the album with the rhythm that propelled its popularity. It was all due to Nile's influence that the album was complete with more funk and more spice. Although *Notorious* did not receive nearly as much hype as anticipated, it showed that the band matured along with its fans.

The mid-eighties was when Duran Duran started to take a different approach with their lyrics, and one could say that they started to appeal to an older audience. The sound had a different arrangement, and their lyrics, in turn, seemed to have more of an effect on those who listened.

Nick recalled that many people compared their new album to dance music, which was in its beginning phases then, and it eventually evolved into the heavy techno that is popular today.

The title track explains the band's exasperation at the press for trying to interfere too much in their lives. After the breakup of The Fab Five, rumours flooded the newspapers. This was a big event in the world of music, and the press wanted to get every piece of information they could.

Of course, this became a great annoyance to the band. Even though Duran Duran still had many loyal fans, their fame had greatly diminished since the breakup. The record company did not write them off because they were still manufacturing their videos and albums.

The other perspective of the argument can be said to be a little against their favour however, because Duran Duran felt that they were not receiving the credit they deserved. Nick claimed that many of Simon's earlier lyrics were metaphysical and sometimes indecipherable. He also compared them to those on *Notorious*, which was overall more realistic. The song, "Skin Trade," served to prove that point because it provides the listener with an example of happenings in everyday life.

While the video for the latter of the two captured the band's charisma, it gave its viewers a different visual style. Duran Duran told their stories through "Notorious" and "Skin Trade." The cameras focused more on what is going on in the background, such as dancing girls and the band as they played their instruments.

To some, it seemed that Duran Duran moved away from the mini movie video format which made their songs famous. The camera shots of the performers and the flying colours tried to fit the new style of music inherent in the album. Even though the band deviated from the previous video format, they were proud of the new style that was present in their videos.

The black and white album cover was inspired by a cover for an Alfred Hitchcock movie, also called *Notorious*. The plot consists of a woman who is asked to spy on a group of Nazis in South America. Although film may not have been a direct inspiration for the album, the band used its cover for the same artistic purposes.

They re-emerged from the ashes of their breakup and proved they had staying power, which allowed them to endure another album. And it would continue to assist them through their new tour.

Unfortunately, this was when the band started to realise that they were going to have a more difficult time selling to their audiences. Shortly after this realisation, John Taylor said that the new trio would have to work harder and show their audience that they had staying power, which guaranteed more to come.

This was a way to promise more to their fans. Despite the fact that many fans still remained loyal through *Notorious*, the remaining members of the band began to worry about their current situation. They were just starting to come to terms with the departure of two of their band members. The trio was not sure how their fans would react to *Notorious* because it was their first album released since the breakup.

Simon made some comments about the production of the album. He asserted that *Notorious* was not much fun to make because they had to set up meetings to deal with the lawyers, who would sort out everything regarding the band's recent loss.

But they also paid tribute to Nile Rodgers to thank him for his great assistance and dedication to the band and their work. *Notorious*, although it contained popular hits such as the title track, "Skin Trade,"

Moving Along

and "Meet El Presidente," didn't do as well as the band's previous albums. The breakup took its toll, causing their interest to diminish. Simon, Nick, and John all agreed that Nile held what was left of Duran Duran together and made their work successful.

John already began his solo career with his first single, "I Do What I Do," which was part of the *9½ Weeks* movie soundtrack, although the alternate version of the song, sung by Lisa Dalbello, was used in the film. The single was a great success. A video followed, which gained the movie even more popularity.

After John went on his own for a while, he was reluctant to regroup with Duran Duran. Nick had to phone him and convince him to come back to England. John decided to go solo while he was touring for The Power Station. During that time, *9½ Weeks* was being produced. One of Michael Des Barres's songs was already being used for the film.

The producers of the movie soon found that they wanted a new song, so John decided to write one. For this project he worked with Jonathan and Michael Elias. He met them through a mutual friend, while Duran Duran was working on the title track, "A View to a Kill."

John also worked with Jonathan Elias on some jazz music, which they hoped would be placed on other movie soundtracks. These tracks were later released on one of John's solo albums, *Resume*.

John had since taken up with a model by the name of Renée Simonsen, but it was around this time that the couple started having problems. While John was in his early to mid-twenties, his mother thought that he was not yet ready to settle down. She advised him to be careful of certain types of women, who were after him for his money.

With the help of her roommate, Renée was able to meet John. When the girl first mentioned Renée, John was not interested. He changed his mind, however, when he found her picture on the cover of *Vogue*. This prompted him to pursue her.

Renée was very happy that the two of them finally got together. She was also the one who wanted to get married, but John responded in the negative. He made the assertion that he was not the marrying type. His opinion about marriage could have changed as a result of Janine's rejection. In between Janine and Renée, he had a brief relationship with a Swedish woman by the name of Chrissie Unstadt.

John said that his work was the main focus of his life. The fact that Renée wanted more of his time, which he was not devoting, had upset her. This distracted her attention away from John, especially

Reach Up For The Sunrise

when other men started to show their interest in her. Renée was at a nightclub when she was charmed by a handsome businessman.

Red flags began to show that John and Renée's relationship was definitely headed for trouble. The couple's stormy relationship resulted in frequent arguments, which sometimes caused Renée to retreat next door to Boy George's apartment. He would console her with cups of coffee while they talked about her troubled relationship with John.

John was always the type to never let adversity defeat him. He found himself faced with many questions regarding the band's new line-up. When asked about the subject, John replied that the new line-up had allowed them to grow and gain musical independence.

The new followers often complained that all their early work sounded the same. Some were critics who had shifted opinions with the recent trade-off. Even though Duran Duran lost the loyal devotion of some of their teenage fans, they gained the respect of the critics who had scoffed at them before.

Some may not have known what to make of *Notorious* at first because it was unlike anything Duran Duran produced before. The album ended up selling over one million copies in the United States, but the record company was hesitant to release any more singles because "Skin Trade" had not done as well as the record executives anticipated.

Even though Simon, Nick, and John were now the face of the band that had seen many personnel changes. One of the most famous new additions was Warren Cuccurullo. While guitar tracks from both he and Andy could be heard on the album, neither one of them were considered to have played lead guitar.

If anyone, Nile Rodgers was associated with that role. The only song which contained guitar music provided by both Andy and Warren was "American Science." The band soon let the public know of their future plans to tour and promote *Notorious*, right after which they would be working on another album.

In August 1986, Andy returned for a brief time, because he was anxious to play guitar for the new album. After he provided a few tracks, however, he refused to do any "serious" work for *Notorious*. Simon tried to convince Andy to re-join, but Andy stuck firm with his decision.

By then, the remaining members (along with Warren), had almost completed *Notorious*. Since Andy was already out of the band, they

Moving Along

didn't have to make any special accommodations for Warren. Andy was still paid for his work on the album. John, Nick, and Simon also realised how distant they had become during the last, few months, and they were glad that Warren was there to fill the void.

Warren Bruce Cuccurullo was born on December 8, 1956 in Canarsie, Brooklyn, to Jerry and Ellen Cuccurullo. He has two brothers, Jerry, commonly known as "Jay," and Robert. He also has two nieces named Nicole and Danielle. Warren was raised in Brooklyn, New York. He was interested in playing drums at a very young age, but it was not long after when he switched his interest over to guitar.

After Warren left school, he worked with his father in his printing business and earned extra cash by giving people guitar lessons. Many of his early musical influences include Led Zeppelin, Jimi Hendrix, Cream, and The Rolling Stones. In the early seventies, Warren became a big fan of Frank Zappa, and he attended every one of his concerts performed close to his home.

As luck would have it, Warren had an opportunity to meet and become friends with Zappa's backing band. They also introduced him to Frank himself. The famous musician introduced Warren to a different lifestyle by having him socialise with another crowd.

One night, while out at a fancy dinner, Warren had the privilege of meeting famous writers William S. Burroughs and Allen Ginsberg. Warren was also pleased that Zappa referred to him as a guitar player to Ginsberg. Warren and Zappa enjoyed another dinner together when they went to Warren's family's house for Thanksgiving. Zappa was so impressed with what he saw that he had a camera crew film the "event" the following year.

In 1978, Warren was invited to a backstage segment to Zappa's concert movie, *Baby Snakes*. It was made for the Halloween shows. Warren toured with Zappa's band in the spring of 1979 for the European tour and spent the rest of the year recording the album, *Joe's Garage*, with the band.

Warren made his debut playing guitar in Frank Zappa's band, and a lot of his work can be heard on *Joe's Garage: Acts I, II and III*, *Shut Up 'n Play Yer Guitar*, *Tinsel Town Rebellion*, and volumes one, four, and six of *You Can't Do That on Stage Anymore*. This was his big start toward fame.

Warren was also known for being in the band Missing Persons, which he had helped form, with founder Terry Bozzio and his then wife,

Dale. The other members included Patrick O'Hearn on synthesizer and bass and Chuck Wild on keyboards. Missing Persons was a band out of Los Angeles, California, formed in 1980.

Dale Bozzio is probably the most memorable member of the band. She was known for her unusual stage costumes. This helped make the band a success. Warren quit Zappa's band to help found Missing Persons. Even though he enjoyed playing up front with the Bozzios, he didn't mind giving up most of the spotlight to Dale, who continued Zappa's trend of introducing him as "Sophia Warren" on stage.

Missing Persons' first album, *Spring Session M* was released in 1982, and it included the hit songs "Destination Unknown" and "Words." The band continued with their line-up of five, until Chuck Wild left after the release of their second album, *Rhyme and Reason*, in 1984. The last album Missing Persons made was *Colour in Your Life*, which was released in 1986. Since then, the members of the band went solo and produced albums of their own. Dale released her solo album *Riot in English* in 1988. The album, however, didn't win much acclaim and is no longer readily available today.

Patrick O'Hearn has produced and released many instrumental albums since 1985. He has also collaborated with many other artists, including Frank Zappa, Rod Stewart, Shankar, and Richard Marx.

After Missing Persons broke up, Warren noticed that Patrick and Terry began to work with Andy Taylor. The three collaborated on their ideas.

When Warren found out that Andy was considering leaving Duran Duran, he pursued the matter by continuously calling the band and sending them tapes of his work. At one point, he even called John and told him that he was their new guitar player. John just laughed it off until his receptionist told them that Andy formed a new band with his backing artists.

It was then when the whole band decided that they were going to take this news a little more seriously. Shortly after the remaining members of Duran Duran found out that Andy was leaving they called Warren in December and hired him.

The other band members may have been perplexed as to why Andy got together with the rhythm section of Missing Persons and a member of the Sex Pistols, Steve Jones. It seemed that since Andy had broken up Warren's band, Warren wanted to return the favour and secure himself a place in Duran Duran.

Moving Along

In 1987, Warren didn't limit himself to Duran Duran. He and his brother Jerry also played on an Epidemics album. Then Warren lent his guitar skills to songs on Patrick O' Hearn's solo albums. He expanded himself further by touring with Tetsuya Komuro in Japan and working with other famous artists such as Meatloaf and Zappa's son Dweezil. Warren also recorded guitar tracks for Michael Jackson's 1996 album, *HIStory: Past, Present and Future, Book I* but unfortunately his work was never used.

The person who took Roger Taylor's place on drums was Steve Ferrone, who remained with the band until 1990. Steve was born in Brighton, England on April 22, 1950. He was educated in France and moved around frequently in his early life. Steve got his first real start in music when he joined the Average White Band in 1974. Others with whom he worked include Climie Fisher, Chaka Khan, and Jaco Pastorius. His solo work includes an album by the name of *It Up*, which was released in 2003.

****

It was not long after Andy left the band when he began to focus on his solo career. Andy began to tour as the opening act for former Van Halen vocalist David Lee Roth. He had seen some success during the beginning of his solo career with the hit single "Take It Easy" from the *American Anthem* soundtrack. This was followed by a busy tour schedule.

The amount of success he acquired was enough for other bands to show interest in his work. Some tried to get him to play guitar for tracks on their albums. Andy worked with a Scottish band called Love and Money and Belinda Carlisle of the Go-Go's. He also co-wrote and played on several songs for Rod Stewart's album, *Out of Order*. It was around this time that he and his wife had their second child, Bethany.

Shortly after writing "Take It Easy" he signed a contract with MCA Records. This was the start of his solo career, and things took off from this point. He was on his way. Andy worked with Steve Jones, of The Sex Pistols, on many other songs for the movie.

Andy cites The Sex Pistols as one of his favourite groups. He remembered seeing them in concert when he was sixteen and recalled that it was one of the best shows he ever attended. He admired Steve's guitar skills and tried to match his ability.

A few years after that, Andy met Steve in San Diego when Jones's band Chequered Past opened for Duran Duran. Andy and Steve formed a great friendship and began to work together after Andy went solo. The two of them toured for Belinda Carlisle's shows on select dates. Andy also pitched in on Belinda Carlisle's solo album by providing guitar for some of her songs.

In 1987, Andy released his first solo album, *Thunder*. It contained songs such as: "I Might Lie," "Tremblin'" and "Don't Let Me Die Young." There were also videos to go along with some of these songs, but they did not receive as much airplay as those he made with Duran Duran.

Andy did a tour to back his new album, but some of his fans came in hopes of hearing songs he made with Duran Duran. While Andy was pleased with the overall production of the album, today he feels that he could have made some changes. He felt the album didn't allow his fans to hear his full potential as an artist.

There were also different instances when Andy found himself bad mouthing the band after he quit. Allegedly, this was after he already took much of the requested time off so that he could focus on his solo works. Despite what he said however, Andy remained on good terms with the remaining members of the Duran Duran.

****

Essentially, Duran Duran's last great tour of the 1980s was the *Strange Behaviour* Tour, which started in 1987 and ended shortly after the start of the following year. Duran Duran went around the world and played a mixture of their big hits from the early part of the decade, and over half the songs from *Notorious*. This provided a great combination of their overly upbeat sound and the new funk handed down by Nile Rodgers.

Despite the great success of the *Strange Behaviour* Tour, fans were disappointed that Andy and Roger had not re-joined the band. While Duran Duran may have suffered from the loss, Nick stated that he didn't want to make any changes because he liked the line-up as it was. Although Warren Cuccurullo was now playing guitar with the band, he wasn't yet recognised as a permanent member. Many fans had yet to learn of his arrival. When they began to notice Warren's presence in the band, a lot of them had mixed reactions.

Moving Along

Warren created a division of opinions from Duran fans. Some welcomed him and thought that he added a new dimension and skill. Others thought that Warren really wasn't really deserving, and they restricted his inclusion in the band.

Regardless of what fans thought, the new guitarist was in the band to take Andy's place. Warren didn't officially declare himself a member of the band until 1989, which was also when Sterling Campbell was officially incorporated, but Warren was featured in small parts of the videos for the band's next two albums.

Preceding some information about the *Strange Behaviour* Tour comes a little history on some of the Duran Duran images and items that became popular during the show. For instance, the origin of the national flag of Duran Duran came from an American article, which stated that Duran Duran was a place rather than a rock group.

The three symbols on Simon's T-shirt worn during many of the shows intrigued audience members. They originally appeared in a film the band made, which was shown during "Save a Prayer." The little globe represents the world; the star signifies the politics that puncture the world, and the heart is what pulls things back together.

The *Strange Behaviour* Tour opened on March 16, 1987 in Japan. A fascinating attribute to the tour was the forty some TV sets that were lifted by hydraulics. The images they showed were very clear, and the fans were delighted at the fact that they could see their favourite band members "up close."

One of the most successful shows was in Paris. It was sold out to thousands and the band surveyed the crowd as they played. The audience lit the arena with the flicker of light from their lighters; this gave the illusion of fireflies hovering in the air. Gifts for the band members were already thrown on stage, just as they were walking out to perform their first number.

They performed three songs, "A View to a Kill," "Notorious," and "American Science" before they even addressed their audience with spoken words. They could tell by the crowd's reaction that the show was going to be successful.

Their play list included a wide diversity of songs from their earlier albums, such as "Planet Earth," "Girls on Film," and "Rio." They also included songs from their side projects, The Power Station's, "Some Like It Hot" and Arcadia's, "Election Day."

Fans were delighted to hear the number one hits produced by

each group. They also wanted to experiment with fragments of other songs, such as The Kingsmen's "Louie Louie," and Sly and the Family Stone's "Dance to the Music," sung by the stage backup singer, Sybil Scoby.

Others who toured with the band, included Steve Nelson on keyboards, Stan Harrison on saxophone, Mac Gollehon playing the horns, and Curtis King, who also sang backing vocals.

When Simon introduced the other members of the band during the song "Hold Me," thousands of fans showed their excitement. The screaming didn't stop until after the band departed the stage to the sound of church bells tolling.

Despite their recent breakup, Duran Duran left 1987 with the success of the tour behind them. The last (and 100th) show of the tour had been a charity gig performed at the Beacon Theatre in New York City. Although the tour was officially over months before, they wanted to leave a lasting impression on their loyal fans.

On January 8, 1988, the band played at the Hollywood Rock Festival in Rio de Janeiro, Brazil. A behind the scenes documentary, called *Three to Get Ready* was released a few months after the tour was completed. It was filmed early in 1987, building up fan's anticipation for the *Strange Behaviour* Tour and directed by David Gasperik. The title, *Three to Get Ready* was a reference to the fact that only three members from the popular line-up still remained in the band.

The documentary is very interesting, as it contains a lot of information about *Notorious*, the upcoming *Strange Behaviour* Tour, and the band after the breakup. Duran Duran started 1988 with great hopes of continuing to seek what they aimed to get back.

CHAPTER 7

Dreaming of a Big Thing

The band's fifth album *Big Thing* was released in 1988. The release of the new album seemed promising on the back of the *Strange Behaviour* Tour. The first single release from the album "I Don't Want Your Love," placed them back at No.49 on the Billboard Hot 100 one week after it was released. The single kept climbing the charts until it finally jumped twenty-five spots after the second week of its release. When "I Don't Want Your Love" reached the No.4 position in the top five, it stayed there for eight weeks until it started to make its way back down.

The second single from the album, didn't do so well in the States. "All She Wants Is" only reached No.22, whereas in the UK the roles were reversed, with the follow-up reaching No.9 whereas "I Don't Want Your Love" only made it to No.14.

The last song on the album, "The Edge of America," was inspired by Peter Gabriel. "Lake Shore Drive" had meaning that is more personal. Simon and John recalled their visits to Lake Shore Drive, located in Chicago. It is a beautiful area surrounded by "concrete beach," which circles the lake.

As was the case with *Notorious*, *Big Thing* contained a different sound. This was the second big change in sound noted by the fans. It moved further away from their roots and expressed more adult-related themes. The band had incorporated a harder rock edge to go along with their lyrics. Mixed in with the hard rock was an element of house music, which was the next stage in the early history of dance music.

Simon liked the idea of incorporating house music in the album and he knew that it was one of the steps that the band had to follow in order to keep up with the changing times. While some fans found that they liked *Big Thing*, the album received a minimal amount of success and was deemed the most disappointing album to date.

As with the previous album, Steve Ferrone provided drums, but in the case of *Big Thing*, drum duties were shared over the tracks with Sterling Campbell.

It only sold a little over 500,000 copies in the United States. This may have been a respectable amount for other groups and artists, but it didn't hold up to the high sales figures generated by earlier Duran Duran records.

When *Big Thing* was released, they kicked off their *Secret Caravan (Caravan Club)* Tour at the Metro Theatre in Chicago. They started to choose more convenient locations for their fans. The fact that there were some more line-up changes going on at the time, however, made more room for scepticism. Those fans, who remained most loyal at the time, felt that they were doing more to please their fan base.

The sixth track off *Big Thing*, "Do You Believe in Shame?" was written by Simon about the death of one of his friends, Dave Miles. The video was directed by Chen Kaige, and it was filmed on the streets of New York City in December 1989.

Unfortunately, the single never took off in the United States, and it was played by very few radio stations and music channels. "Do You Believe in Shame?" was the first of three songs written for the late Dave Miles and reached its highest point on the U.S. Billboard charts at No.72. In England, the song reached No.25 and was moving up as of May 1, 1990. Because of lack of airplay in the United States, the song kept sliding down the charts and eventually fell out of the top 100.

The videos became more distinct, especially the one for "All She Wants Is" which included the same camera technology featured in "Missing," one of the lesser-known songs by Arcadia. Dean Chamberlain provided the unique visuals for both of the videos by using unique lighting effects; he painted around the models while they had to stand still for five hours.

While some fans felt that Duran Duran may have been testing their limits regarding further experimentation, its members were just as pleased with their work and claimed they had no regrets. "I Don't Want Your Love" told a story through a courtroom drama, while more colours flashed in the background. In between were shots of them performing the song and actors following the story with choreography.

At this point, the band went back to their narrative element, of telling stories within their songs. The video for "All She Wants Is" explored new camera technology, which added vibrancy to the story and made it come to life before the very eyes of its viewers.

Nick didn't let the band's diminishing fame upset him. He claimed that he felt relieved because of the wane in popularity from what was known as their "heyday." According to the keyboard player, during their earlier days, he said that what they represented at the time was false, suggesting superficiality among the "fair weather fans."

Nick also asserted that Duran Duran felt they were in a better position because they had more time to reflect on their work and themselves. Duran Duran was relieved to find that they survived the success they had during their heyday.

They were also proud of the fact that they had sold five to six million copies of *Big Thing* worldwide. The album still made its way into the Billboard Top 40, which led some of their listeners to believe that they were still fighting to regain the heights of their early fame.

The fact that the album fared relatively well did not necessarily mean that everyone was pleased. John admitted that he was ready to quit the band due to a fight they had over the song "Drug." He wanted to include the original version on the album, but the rest of the band didn't agree with his decision. Instead, the track was included on the "Do You Believe in Shame?" limited edition triple pack, including three records and three black and white postcards. "Drug (It's Just a State of Mind) Original Version" is the final track on the third record.

The B-side lasted almost seven full minutes, but John felt that the album was nearly incomplete without the inclusion of that mix. Simon added that Duran Duran had aged, and the band's lyrics were blunter because they started to say what they really felt. They became true to themselves as artists.

Duran Duran also hired a new manager, Peter Rudge, who had also worked with groups such as The Rolling Stones and The Who. When Andy and Roger left in 1985, they had also parted ways with Paul and Michael Berrow.

The brothers were given a ninety-day notice, which caused a lot of fighting and lawsuits on both sides. Harsh words were exchanged, and the Berrows severed contact with most of the band. The only one who remains on speaking terms with the brothers was Simon. Since Paul and Michael were out of the picture, this left the band open to move in another direction.

While Duran Duran was struggling at the time, Yasmin was at

the peak of her career. She appeared on the covers of various fashion and glamour magazines, such as *Vogue*. Yasmin was also featured on the runway in fashion shows around the world. She modelled for famous designers such as Calvin Klein and Christian Dior. Yasmin's popularity was increasing so much that she was becoming almost as well-known as top supermodels, such as Cindy Crawford.

In 1989, between *Big Thing* and *Liberty* came the compilation album *Decade*. It contained the band's greatest hits from 1981-1989. Included on this album were the singles "The Wild Boys," and "A View to a Kill." At the time of its release, "A View to a Kill" was released as a separate single — not included on any of the albums.

Decade featured a cover with photographs of the band by Stephen Sprouse, who was known for his works of art incorporated into fashion. One of his other famous works included a pair of pants he made for Debbie Harry of Blondie. Stephen Sprouse passed away in 2003.

A single released to coincide with *Decade*, but not included on the album, was "Burning the Ground." The song spanned the band's career up to that point and featured segments of their greatest hits.

"Burning the Ground" originally came from a suggestion made to Nick. The label came up with the idea to remix one of their greatest hits, but Nick wasn't too fond of the suggestion. He wanted to do something better that would recapture the interest of wayward fans. The band went into the studio and played around with many sounds from their hits until they finally had enough material to build their new single. At that time, another song called "Decadance" was released.

Just as "Burning the Ground," it contained portions of their early hits. While they were pleased with the outcome of the song, some of their fans didn't share their enthusiasm. *Decade*, at its best, only made it to No.67 on Billboard but it reached No.5 in the UK.

****

In 1989, Jonathan Elias recorded and produced an album to benefit Native Americans. It was titled *Requiem for the Americas: Songs from the Lost World*, and it featured great works by many artists. The album is considered a rock tribute. It was inspired by the photographic work of Edward S. Curtis, whose photographs depicted the life of Native Americans taken around the turn of the century.

One unforgettable song from the album included a duet called

"Follow in My Footsteps." It was sung by Simon and Susanna Hoffs of the Bangles. Elias also contributed many works of his own, some of which included "The Journey/The Chant Movement," (for which John played bass) and "Far Far Cry," which also features Jon Anderson of Yes. During the beginning of the song, one can also hear the late Jim Morrison recite his poetry.

Other artists featured on the album include Grace Jones and Toni Childs. Warren Cuccurullo and Steve Ferrone also contributed music for the album. John Taylor helped promote the album in Europe, and it was released in record stores shortly after.

****

Ever since Nick Rhodes and Andy Warhol met, they always had an admiration for each other. In 1989, Nick was offered a chance to play the part of Andy Warhol on an American TV movie. The film was a project documentary describing the Pittsburgh native's life. He was eager to take on the role, until he read the script.

Nick felt that the depiction was not accurate. He was upset by the fact that those who wrote the script didn't focus on Warhol's life as an artist. Most of the emphasis was placed on his personal life. Nick doesn't regret his decision by refusing the role because he felt he did the right thing by sticking to what he believed.

1989 was also a sad year for John and Renée, as the pair split up. The fact that John didn't want to get married and have children, while Renée did, caused the breakup.

John said that he felt he needed to be single again, as he thought his fan status had dipped since he took Renée as his girlfriend. As a result of the breakup, however, John moped around his apartment, ordered pizzas, and watched TV. Although he was morose about the breakup, it didn't take very long for him to move on.

Around this time, Andy had fallen out of contact with the rest of the band. He lived in Spain with Tracey and their three children. Not much was reported on him during that time. Andy kept himself and his family out of the media, mostly for the protection of his children. He was a bit like Roger in the respect that he enjoyed the solitude of a more private life. This gave him more time to spend with his family, doing the things that he loved.

His second solo album, *Dangerous*, was released in 1990. It was a covers album that consisted of hit songs, such as The Kinks' "Lola," Mack Rice's "Mustang Sally," and Thins Lizzy's "Don't Believe a Word." He also covered "Be Good to Yourself," which was written by Andy Fraser of Free and had been a hit for Frankie Miller. This was released on the b-side of the 12" "Lola" single.

Due to the previous wane in his solo career, *Dangerous* won him little acclaim. That was why he decided he would cover songs that inspired him during his younger days. Between *Thunder* and *Dangerous*, Andy released singles such as "Dead on the Money" and "Suffragette City," the latter by David Bowie.

In 1991, Andy and Luke Morley of Thunder recorded four songs on a rare CD known as the *Spanish Sessions*. The four songs were "Can't Stop the Rain," "Lightning," "Quiet Life," and "Sleeping with the Past."

Roger released two 12" singles of techno tracks on the RT Music label under the name of Funk Face — rare collector's items for any Duranie.

****

On August 3, 1990, Duran Duran released their seventh studio album, *Liberty*, which did worse than anticipated. The album more or less failed, especially in the United States, where it only reached No.46. The album made it to No.8 in the UK.

Liberty was mostly recorded at Stanbridge Farm Studios in Sussex. The sessions resulted in songs that were the first things that came to their minds.

The album was originally going to be called *Low and Slow*, but they soon decided to change the name to *Liberty*. There was a concerted effort to get *Liberty* out to the stores as soon as possible. The album was originally due out in the spring, but the production took longer than anticipated. Some of the song titles were also changed.

"Read My Lips" was formerly named "Second Alibi," "My Antarctica" used to be called "Throb," and "Yo Bad Azzizi" was known as "Nuclear War" when it was performed for the first time in 1989. "Yo Bad Azzizi" was originally intended to be included on the album, but it didn't make the cut, so it was released as a single.

Simon admitted to the fact that the band was not paying much attention to the songs they recorded because preoccupation got the better of them. He does, however, find pride in some of the songs, such as "Serious" and "My Antarctica" because more thought was put into the lyrics.

Simon went on to say that the album was not necessarily a bad product, but the band knew it was lacking in certain spots on some of the other songs. Even though new technology enabled them to create interesting sounds effects for their music, audiences' attentions were shifting to the new bands.

Grunge rock saw its beginnings. It was played extensively on college radio. Popular grunge rockers at the time included Nirvana, Alice in Chains, Pearl Jam, and Jane's Addiction. These bands were very quick to rise to fame. These new sounds soon dominated the charts and airwaves. As a result of this, *Liberty* was not stocked in many stores until it was reissued some years later.

The one successful single yielded from the album was "Serious," which was aired on MTV for a short time. "Violence of Summer (Love's Taking Over)" was the other single from the album, but it achieved less airplay although it did manage to struggle its way to the top twenty on the UK charts, but it got nowhere near that in the United States, where it didn't even make it into the top 50.

The strong images in the video reflect the plot, which consists of one man stealing another's woman, and putting himself in danger. He eventually ended up being beaten and left in the woods. Here one considers the title of the song, which suggests the violence of the situation. Themes of eroticism are also present in the video as scantily clad women seduce the cameras.

For the most part, John was pleased with the video, and he liked what the producers at Big TV had done. John also admitted that he didn't like much of what he saw on MTV at the time, although he felt that the band should try and make a video to please the masses. Grunge rock changed the climate of the music scene, and many younger people found themselves interested in this new movement.

Duran Duran was also pleased with what they called the "relationship songs" on the albums because of their metaphors and the way they applied themselves to their listeners. Songs of social relevance were also important to the band and the critics who listened to their most recent works.

The song "Read My Lips" was inspired by President H. W. Bush's catch phrase. It urged its listeners to ease their minds and not resist what was being thrown at them through popular media.

Another track off *Liberty*, "Hothead," included snippets of President Bush's voice. The piece is actually an indictment of CNN presenting an American view on the world, which was the general assumption of how things were at the time. John and the other members of the band agreed that such a narrow viewpoint could lead to potential danger when no one else is being considered.

Those who listened to the album may have noticed that these new songs were urging people to think on another level. Members of the band maintained that they have been able to stay together because they had placed the utmost importance on pleasing themselves with their works. After all, if Duran Duran wasn't pleased with what they had done, then their fans would feel the same way.

The world had entered a new decade, and much of the older music was no longer popular. The radio stations played a lot of music that was categorised as either dance or hard rock. Since Duran Duran didn't fit into either of these categories, they had a difficult time getting any radio play for their new singles.

Technology began to play an important part in new music. The dance music that was frequently played on the radio gained popularity because of the new sounds and beats that were incorporated into the music. Popular groups in the dance category included KLF and Technotronic.

Duran Duran knew how important technology became and they tried to keep on top of these advances. One who listens to *Liberty* can observe the new sounds with which the band experimented. Sterling Campbell who replaced Steve Ferrone on drums was responsible for making these new sounds fit into the album and his experimentation was successful. He was signed on as a permanent member, although he would leave the band before the release of their next album.

Sterling was born on May 3, 1964 in New York City and he graduated from LaGuardia High School. He got a start on his musical career in the 1980s when he began to work with Cyndi Lauper. As soon as John had moved Renée out, he offered to let Sterling live with him in his house in Ennismore.

Other artists with whom Sterling worked with include Soul Asylum, Tina Turner, The B-52s, and David Bowie. This was also when Warren was fully credited as a permanent member of the band. Warren also began to collaborate by providing some of the song lyrics.

Nick felt that the band did a good job on the production of *Liberty*. Many fans, however, were more disappointed in *Liberty* than they were in *Big Thing*. It was hard for the band to accept this as a failure. Due to the album's poor sales they decided not to promote the album with a tour.

Interest waned to the point that the record company thought any effort of revival would be futile. Also, the band thought the tour wouldn't be profitable. The bottom line always rules in the music industry. This was the first time that the band didn't follow a new album with a tour.

By the time the 1990 MTV Music Awards was aired, Duran Duran was in Los Angeles, promoting *Liberty*. Famous performers, such as Aerosmith and Janet Jackson, won many awards in different categories. Unfortunately, Duran Duran was not even part of the award ceremony that year. They all wanted to attend the show, but they couldn't even get tickets. This is just one example of how the band's fame waned by the end of 1990.

But Duran Duran was never the type to give up. Once they had it in their minds that they wanted to do something, they got it done. Even though their fans dwindled down to a smaller number, the band still had their faithful followers. Their music had simply changed with the coming of the new decade.

One intriguing thing about the cover of *Liberty* is the photography, which is also shown inside the booklet of the CD. The pictures were taken by Ellen Von Unwerth at Foire du Trone, an amusement park in Paris. The two women featured on the cover worked on the album with the band and were shown in both videos. They were known as Italian girl, Sylvia and Dutch girl, Claudia.

In 1991, Simon Le Bon had a serious motorcycle accident. He crashed his Yamaha 400cc on a track in Wales. Simon flew over the handlebars, landed, and crushed his testicles in the process. As a result, the doctors had to surgically remove one of them because it was damaged beyond repair. Just as what happened with the Drum, the accident did not deter Simon because he loved motorbikes too much to give them up.

Yasmin also began to gain more fame this year, as she appeared on the cover of *Hello* Magazine several times. The first article featured the birth of their first daughter, Amber Rose, in 1989. Nearly a year later, the same type of article was written when Saffron was born.

Probably the most well-known of these issues covered Yasmin's trip to South America to encourage and demonstrate ecological devotion. She was six months pregnant with Saffron at the time. About two weeks before she embarked upon her journey, she had a nude photograph of herself taken. It was sold to the highest bidder at an auction, who was none other than her husband.

John also got married that year. A beautiful, young woman by the name of Amanda de Cadenet became the envy of his large female following.

On Christmas Eve 1991, the day of their wedding, their marriage vows were sealed at the Chelsea Register Office with a simple ceremony. Only fifteen guests were included — close relations and friends of the couple. Amanda was five months pregnant at the time of their wedding. Despite that some may have thought, that was not the only reason why they chose to get married. John suggested Christmas Eve for their wedding day because it meant that their friends and families would be able to attend the ceremony.

Even though the wedding was small, there were many details that needed to be taken care of. Since Amanda was already five months along with their child, she had an extremely difficult time trying to find a dress that would fit her. Few of them came in designs that she liked.

To make matters worse, she was so rushed on her wedding day that she was pulled over by a police officer for speeding. Even after she explained her situation to him, he made her go to the station and watch a video of her speeding. Not only was the incident humiliating, but it cost her a lot of time. Amanda finally got to the register office, on time, but she was still upset by the whole event. In addition to this a girl had falsely claimed that she was going to have John's baby.

John and Amanda met in 1989, when she was only seventeen. They went to see a play starring Julie Anne. This was around the same time that Amanda was getting ready to launch her TV career at the satellite station BSB. She was on her second series of Channel 4's *The Word*.

Amanda is the daughter of race car driver Alain de Cadenet. Her mother, Anna, is an interior designer. Her parents divorced when she was nine and by then she was already considered a wild child. Amanda was dancing on tabletops at various clubs by the time she was fourteen. She was not afraid to experiment with certain things. Amanda was living her life to the fullest, whether or not her actions were condoned.

Dreaming of a Big Thing

****

By this time, Andy put his solo career far behind him and began working with bands he was producing out of his own studio, Trident Studios. Andy's proud work ethic was emphasised as he embarked upon these projects. It was around this time that Andy collaborated with Rod Stewart. The two of them co-produced with Bernard Edwards's band, Out of Order, on their comeback album.

Prior to reuniting with Duran Duran, Andy had kept himself busy as a producer, working on average on five albums per year. He mostly worked with British metal bands. Andy also produced an album by the Scottish band Big Country.

Reach Up For The Sunrise

Friends of many, the five-man line-up in 1981.
(Pictorial Press Ltd / Alamy Stock Photo)

Young boys in Philadelphia, PA in 1982.
(MediaPunch Inc / Alamy Stock Photo)

The fab five line-up during their prime youth, 1983.
(IconicPix / Alamy Stock Photo)

John, Simon, and Andy in the futuristic world of 1984.
(AF archive / Alamy Stock Photo)

Duran Duran's Strange Behaviour at Wembley Arena in 1987.
(ilpo musto / Alamy Stock Photo)

Nick tries to capture an early selfie of himself, Simon, Sterling Campbell, Warren, and John in a break from rehearsals at the London Arena at Limeharbour in London's Docklands in 1989.
(PA Images / Alamy Stock Photo)

Pilgrim's progress?
Nick, Simon, and John in 1989.
(Trinity Mirror / Mirrorpix / Alamy Stock Photo)

Nick, Simon, Warren, and John around the time of Liberty, 1990.
(INTERFOTO / Alamy Stock Photo)

Does it have to be serious?
Warren, Simon, and John in 1990.
(dpa picture alliance / Alamy Stock Photo)

Andy Taylor remaining solo
in 1991.
(David Bagnall / Alamy Stock Photo)

Duran Duran in 1993, shortly after the release of The Wedding Album.
(dpa picture alliance / Alamy Stock Photo)

The five-man line-up enjoying their second wave of fame at the Roxy in West Hollywood, California in 2003.
(Francis Specker / Alamy Stock Photo)

Nick and Warren attending the Grand Opening Celebration of the Hard Rock Hotel, Las Vegas, Nevada before they were bored with Prozac and the Internet, 1995.
(Barry King / Alamy Stock Photo)

Last chance on the stairway? Simon and Nick backstage at the Jay Leno Show in 2004. (Trinity Mirror / Mirrorpix / Alamy Stock Photo)

Simon, Nick, John, Andy, and Roger reaching up for the sunrise in 2004.
(Yui Mok, PA Images / Alamy Stock Photo)

Wild Boys John, Simon, and Dom Brown front and centre at the Ultra Music Festival in Miami, Florida in 2011.
(Corey Weiner, Red Square Photography / Alamy Stock Photo)

The members of Duran Duran ready for South Park's 15 Anniversary party in 2011.
(Everett Collection Inc / Alamy Stock

Simon dressed like a dapper gent at the 2011 Brit Awards at the O2 Arena, London.
(Yui Mok, PA Images / Alamy Stock

Epic guitar and bass battle between Don and John at Citibank Hall in Rio de Janeiro in 2012. (Néstor J. Beremblum / Alamy Stock Photo)

Andy Hamilton, Simon, and John at the 2015 Life Is Beautiful Festival in Las Vegas.
(Yaacov Dagan / Alamy Stock Photo)

John Taylor walking to the BBC Studios in Manchester, 2015 for an appearance on Breakfast.
(WENN Rights Ltd / Alamy Stock Photo)

The four-man line-up shortly after the release of Paper Gods, 2015.
(MARKA / Alamy Stock Photo)

Duran Duran headlined the finale of BBC Music Day at the Eden Project, Cornwall, June 2016. Dom playing with fire without getting burned!
(Simon Maycock / Alamy Stock Photo)

CHAPTER 8

Knock, Knock, Remember Us?

For Duran Duran 1993 would prove to be an important year when they made a huge comeback with the colossal hits "Ordinary World" and "Come Undone" from their second self-titled album — *The Wedding Album* — as many came to know it, because it featured the wedding pictures of the band members' parents on the front cover.

Also, John thought of his and Amanda's wedding when making the album, which some might have seen as a "shotgun wedding." The band also named one of their instrumental tracks, "Shotgun," after the notion.

At one point, John joked that they were going to call their new album "The Right Album" as a play on words in reference to The Beatles' "The White Album." They may have hoped that fans would think the same way and renew their interest in the band. Some who lost interest in their music after the breakup found themselves turning on their radios and searching for all their old Duran Duran records that they hadn't listened to since the eighties. Durandamonium was happening again, as many of these fans rediscovered their "old" fascination.

"Ordinary World" came in at No.20 on the Adult Contemporary and Modern Rock Tracks charts four weeks after it was released. It also made the Top 10 in both the U.S. and the U.K. "Ordinary World" was also the second song written about the loss of his dear friend, David Miles.

The lyrics were such that those who empathised with the situation could come to terms with themselves and carry on with their own lives. "Ordinary World" illustrates man's will to survive, the very thing that Simon had seen working as a hospital porter years earlier. The video matches the theme of the song. The first camera shot is of a bride and groom being photographed. Then, they show the bride walking away from "fate" to try and discover her own life.

When they later looked back and remembered that "Ordinary World" was their saving grace. In 1991, Capitol EMI said that they would give the band an advance on their new album. The band had met with the company's president, Rupert Perry, in Manchester Square, London. This was on the condition that if they liked the "new hit" that Duran Duran produced, they would give them more money for the album. Needless to say, the song was a great success, and it helped the band tremendously.

"Come Undone" reached No.10 in the States. The song was written about the troubled lives people lead. In the video, some shots focus on the band playing by a large aquarium. The others zoom in on the troubled individuals, many who do not see much reason to live.

At the same time, a woman is underwater, and she tries to free herself from the chains that bind her. This represents the struggle undergone by those people with their troubled lives and the constant battle to set themselves free. In the end, the woman rids herself of her chains, but she eventually comes undone.

Some try to delve even further into the meaning and say that it's a love song, but Simon likes to maintain that it's "purely a sex song." Whatever the case, fans find that they cannot undermine its meaning, even if they make their own. It's all a matter of interpretation.

Part of the video also won Duran Duran a brief moment of fame in the world of animation when it was featured on the popular MTV cartoon, *Beavis and Butt-Head*. After the two animated morons "evaluated" the video, they seemed to like it, which was more than they did for Missing Person's video for "Words," as they watched that one for less than a minute.

The third single from the album was "Too Much Information," which criticised MTV for mass marketing too much to the general public. While Duran Duran didn't want to "bite the hand that feeds them," they felt they had to get their point across. The video features a live performance by the band thrown in with the video performance and various clips of old movies and TV shows.

If one pays close attention, they can also see a few video clips from "The Chauffeur" towards the end. The video audience members, all wearing 3-D glasses, represent the consumers, who are soaking up the information with which they are bombarded.

Soon, however, the band and the music network kissed and made up. MTV showed more clips of the band's music. Other popular songs from the album included "Breath After Breath," and a cover of "Femme Fatale." "Femme Fatale" was originally written by Lou Reed and sung by Nico.

While they enjoyed covering the song, they got the idea from Frank Zappa, who suggested it to Warren. "Breath After Breath" was filmed in Buenos Aires and included clips from the performance they held there.

Interestingly enough, the majority of *The Wedding Album* was recorded in the living room of Warren's London home, which had been leased to him by Simon and Yasmin once they moved back into their own house.

All songs were written and arranged by the band except for "Breath After Breath." The song was written by Brazilian composer, Milton Nascimento, who provided some of the vocals. Warren's girlfriend at the time, Brazilian model Claudia Bueno, briefly appears in the video. Her son, Mayko, is the young boy who is featured in some of the shots.

"Ordinary World" may have been popular for more than one reason. While many fans argue that it was the most successful single off the album, it does not mean that people were anxious to hear it before its release. "Ordinary World's" early release attracted the attention of an alternative radio station, KROQ-FM. in Los Angeles. This helped the song reach the No.1 position coast to coast.

Sterling Campbell had already left in 1991, and Steve Ferrone briefly re-joined. His work appears on "Ordinary World," and "Too Much Information." Some may find it ironic that Steve came back to play for two of the three most popular songs from the album.

Both Nick and John had made comments about their newly acquired success. They based them on the thought that things which went out of style had a tendency to come back into the mainstream. Rob Gordon, of Capitol Records, also made the assertion that it was the right time for the band to come back into the spotlight.

Nick again alluded to the dwindling fame that faced the band before the release of *The Wedding Album*. He says they resigned themselves to thinking that they had a cult following, consisting mainly of college students who were fans since the eighties. It was easy for the members of the band to come to this conclusion, especially since they had not made a top 40 single since 1989, with the release of *Decade*.

As mentioned before, Sterling Campbell left and joined a new band called Soul Asylum, best known for their hit song, "Runaway Train." He was a member of Soul Asylum from 1995 to 1998. This was also around the time that Campbell was featured on the cover of *Rolling Stone* Magazine.

A few years into the decade, he changed his faith to follow a spiritual movement known as the Falun Gong. It is a traditional Chinese movement, which has elements similar to Buddhism and Taoism. Campbell joined the movement in hopes that it would help him conquer his problem with substance abuse, of which he was a victim for years.

In February 2002, Campbell and some other followers attended a peaceful protest in China despite their religion having been banned by the Chinese government. He was arrested and detained until a later sentence included expulsion from the country.

Despite the loss of a recent member, Duran Duran was nowhere near ready to admit defeat. Their future plans involved moving on to the next big thing. Any doubts which the lads had about their abilities disappeared after they recorded with Warren in the studio. He provided phenomenal guitar for all the tracks on *The Wedding Album*, especially his work on "Ordinary World" and "Come Undone."

Also, these songs had more of an alternative sound, which was growing in popularity because of its similarities to grunge rock. John made the comment that Duran Duran began second-guessing themselves around the time when they thought things first went wrong.

This is why they thought their most recent albums failed. Duran Duran decided to put the most effort possible into this work, which would be different from the half-hearted attempts they had made in the past. Since they had learned from the mistakes of their last album, Duran Duran knew that they had the ability to recapture their fans' interest, which accounted for their newly recreated success.

Shortly after *The Wedding Album* was released they parted ways with manager Peter Rudge. Nick made the claim that the split was mutual, saying that both Rudge and the band ran each other into the ground and that they were due for a change, which would lead them into different career directions.

Left Bank Management took over business affairs and along with the band mutually decided to delay the release of the album for a further six months.

Through all the excitement surrounding the eventual release of

The Wedding Album, the band felt as if they were releasing their newest work all over again. Nick maintained that the fans simply needed motivation to revive their interest. Not only did the band need to re-establish their old fan base and open the door for new devotees, but they also had to convince the press and critics that they were worthy of the attention their hard work would gain for them.

After a marketing strategy was implemented, Capitol Records wanted to bring forward the album's release date in the United States. This couldn't happen, however, because agreements for simultaneous international release were signed. In turn, the extra time taken to perfect the album and all the radio promotion that it received served to benefit the band. John Fagot, the senior vice president of promotion, wanted to make sure that the band and the album had exactly what they needed in order to succeed.

For the lads, longevity was the most important aspect of the project. John Fagot predicted many good things would come after the worldwide release of *The Wedding Album*. One result of this was that "Ordinary World" gained popularity so fast that the band had to catch up and make a video for the song.

By June, "Ordinary World" reached No.7 on the Billboard top 200 chart. In England, it placed a little higher by reaching No.4. It also made the charts in Japan, the Philippines, Taiwan, Singapore, Malaysia, Hong Kong, Venezuela, Mexico, Brazil, South Africa, New Zealand, and Australia.

The band received many congratulations on the success of *The Wedding Album*, which went platinum in Argentina; this was the first time such a milestone had been achieved. The album also sold more than one million copies in the United States, which was a vast improvement compared to their sales for *Big Thing* and *Liberty*. Despite what some of the members of the band previously said, they were relieved to have achieved their renewed success, which was nearly eight years in the making.

On November 17, 1993, they performed at Sony Music Studios in New York. The performance was for MTV Unplugged, which has aired on both that channel and VH1. The set list included "Hungry Like the Wolf," "Ordinary World," "Serious," "Girls on Film," "Rio," "Planet Earth," "Come Undone," "Too Much Information," "Skin Trade," "The Chauffeur," and "Notorious."

Some twists were put on these songs, giving them an almost

entirely new sound. One could say that they had both a folky and ethnic feel at the same time, a far cry from the pop sound which had made the band famous.

Others who contributed to the performance included the talent of John Jones, Andy Gangadeen, Fergus Gerrand, Curtis King, Lamya, Yolisa Phahle, Ellen Blair, Ivan Hussey, Mineko Yajima, Carol Poole, and Mike Takayama.

The performance was also released as an unofficial album, containing three live, bonus tracks, "Crystal Ship," "Ordinary World," and "Starting to Remember." These were compiled from various live performances from 2000.

1993 was a good year for Duran Duran. Not only did they enjoy their "newfound" fame, but they also received a star on the Hollywood Walk of Fame. This attracted the attention of many of their newest fans. This was also the year when they filmed a documentary called *ExtraOrdinary World* (released in 1994). It was directed, written, and produced by Allie Eberhardt.

Like most other documentaries, the band is interviewed as they all talk about their beginnings, success, ups and downs, and future directions. What I liked most about *ExtraOrdinary World*, however, is the fact that lots of visual images were thrown in to coincide with the band members as they were talking.

Although the second part of the VHS tape contained a few of their videos from *Liberty* and *The Wedding Album*, I liked the fact that they showed large portions of videos from their older albums as they talked about their inspiration and what the band was going through at the time. Just with any good film, the visuals aid the rest of the art. To me, as well as many other Duranies, this made the document all the more interesting.

Two members of the band made what was their debut in fashion on June 9, 1993 when they starred with Cindy Crawford on MTV's *House of Style*. Not only did Simon and Nick make interesting wardrobe suggestions for Cindy, but they also came out of the dressing rooms, wearing pink and white frocks. Nick was still wearing his trousers underneath.

Despite these light-hearted moments, however, not everyone could escape the woes of their personal lives. Nick and his wife Julie Ann had officially divorced because of irreconcilable differences. (They originally split around 1990.) The couple had one daughter, Tatjana

Lee Orchid.

The divorce grew more turbulent when the two of them battled over who would have custody of Tatjana. It was mainly for the sake of Tatjana that Nick and Julie Ann remained friends. Their divorce was not necessarily acrimonious, but they had found that their lives were moving in different directions.

For a while after the divorce, Julie Ann and Tatjana lived in the house that the couple bought when they were first married. Nick moved into the house beside them, so he could stay close and visit with his daughter whenever he wanted. Julie Ann eventually went back to the United States and became a chef, for which she is primarily known today.

Shortly after the divorce was finalised, Nick started dating Madeline Farley. The two had met at a party the previous year. Nick said the thing that attracted him to Madeline was her great sense of humour. When the two of them met, their personalities matched, but Nick still felt that something wasn't right.

There were some things that Nick felt Madeline needed to change. Her wardrobe consisted of baggy and unflattering clothes. She also didn't wear any makeup. He decided to work his magic as "Pygmalion" when he changed Madeline's appearance from grungy to glamorous. After he worked on her physical appearance, he gave her an education in the arts by introducing her to some of his favourite films and directors.

Although Nick transformed Madeline, she came into his life when he needed someone the most. He was still vulnerable from the divorce, and Madeline provided for his emotional needs. Since Nick knew that his marriage was through, he felt that he needed another companion.

As the members of the band grew older, they realised that some of their sex appeal had worn off. They didn't let such a trivial thing get in their way, however, because they focused primarily on their business. Nick made the statement that he was never one to take such things seriously. He proved that he wasn't going to let this hinder the band's progress.

Another thing the band had to take into consideration was the fact that the fans grew older themselves, and some of them had returned to the concerts with their husbands, wives, and/or children. Since these older fans essentially followed their career from the beginning, they generated such warmth that the younger fans may have lacked.

These fans knew that things were a bit rough, and they hoped that the band knew they had their undying support. John Taylor stated that if Duran Duran was a single person, they would have lost their fame years ago, but the fact that they are a band enabled them to communicate and collaborate on their ideas. This helped them through and saw them to their newly relived fame.

The Wedding Album, however, also received some negative criticism from opinionated reviewers and sceptics alike. Many critics didn't like the last three songs on the album, "Shelter," "To Whom It May Concern," and "Sin of the City." "Sin of the City" concerned a tragic incident that occurred at a club called Happy Land in New York City. It burned to the ground on March 25, 1990.

Eighty-seven (although the songs says eighty-nine) people died from the fire, and only five survived. Had the owners of the club not violated safety code procedures, the horrible incident might never have happened. Despite what many critics had to say about their album, Duran Duran took any criticism in stride.

Simon made a profound point by stating that some of the most famous works through time have received bad reviews. For instance, the classic novel, *Wuthering Heights*, by Emily Brönte was considered less than average at the time of its publication and received very little literary praise. This was also the case with most of the works of William Shakespeare. At best, his plays were considered very low brow during the time of their original performances. Now, Shakespeare is the most canonised writer in the English language.

As time goes by, those who did not like *The Wedding Album* before might, in the future, appreciate its appeal. In most cases of whether something is good or not, it's merely a matter of opinion. To paraphrase an old adage, everyone has an opinion, and if we all agreed on everything, things would be pretty boring.

Following the great success of the album were the tours for 1993 and 1994. Terrance Trent D'Arby was the opening act in the States. Most of the shows were acoustic, but they were still able to generate a phenomenal amount of success. This was enough to have their fans craving more shows.

In October 1994, a minor setback occurred, delaying the tour dates. Simon was diagnosed with a torn vocal cord after a performance in Bethlehem, Pennsylvania. The tour was postponed indefinitely, while Simon remained under the care of throat doctors in Manhattan.

The rest of the band remained in Los Angeles and awaited his return. With antibiotics, his condition improved in a little over two weeks. Luckily, he didn't suffer any permanent damage, although his voice became higher as a result. The tour picked up soon after and continued as planned.

Extra performers in the tour line-up included singer Lamya Al-Mugheiry, formerly of the group Soul II Soul, and Fergus Gerrand, who replaced Sterling Campbell on drums. *The Wedding Album* was a strong example of just how much staying power Duran Duran had, which brought them to the new decade. Warren Cuccurullo still played lead guitar, which made it seem like a new era with great possibilities for continued fame.

Despite the album's great success, Simon suffered writer's block. This remained with him until it was time to begin work on their next album.

Reach Up For The Sunrise

CHAPTER 9

Covering Others

In 1995, Duran Duran released their ninth studio album, *Thank You*. It consist of cover songs from artists such as Lou Reed, The Doors, Led Zeppelin, Elvis Costello, and Grandmaster Flash and the Furious Five. Some of the songs on the album were written by bands who inspired them during their youth. *Thank You* was their way of paying homage to these bands.

One of the most fascinating songs on the album is a version of The Doors' "Crystal Ship," which starts with Simon singing in a baritone key, similar to Jim Morrison's, before he makes the transition into his normal singing voice. Simon acknowledges The Doors as one of his favourite bands. He was quoted as saying that he wanted to be like Jim Morrison when he was on stage. Simon also stated that The Doors were one of Duran Duran's early influences. Nick also stated he has an affinity for them.

An original track recorded for *Thank You* is called "Drive By." It includes Simon recording poetry while an instrumental version of "The Chauffeur" played in the background. Another song that was rumoured to have been recorded was "Lithium" by Nirvana since they heard the news of Kurt Cobain's suicide and recorded it as a tribute to the late singer. However they weren't sure whether to include it on the album and they eventually decided not to.

They started recording the album in the summer of 1994, not long after their previous tour ended. Nick recalled being disappointed that *Thank You* had not done as was well as they anticipated. It barely made the top twenty in the United States and fared little better in the United Kingdom.

Thank You also contained a song called "White Lines," which was the biggest single from the album. A video was made which included the original performers of the song, Grandmaster Flash and

Reach Up For The Sunrise

the Furious Five. The video contained a different version of the song than what was on the album. This was also Simon's first public attempt at rapping. The song primarily serves as a warning against the use of cocaine, the same substance which John Taylor had abused.

There was no tour for *Thank You* because John entered rehab to try and conquer his addiction. Shortly after Duran Duran became famous, John became addicted to cocaine. His overall health and relationships were adversely affected. It especially took a toll on his relationship with Nick, which, thankfully was mended.

John was briefly romantically involved with pop singer, Kim Wilde, but she left him shortly after she found out about his addiction. Stories such as these always made the news, and any bad press a band member received generated much concern from their family members. Although they hoped none of what they had read was true, they found out otherwise. Slowly, John got over his addiction, and he remains drug free today.

Despite the mixed reactions and reviews *Thank You* received, the guys were proud of the work they did with the album. Aside from carefully taking each song into consideration, they felt there was only so much they could change because every song had at least one element that made it a classic.

When Lou Reed heard the remake he made the assertion that it was better than his own version. He also stated that it should have been recorded their way in the first place. Whatever liberties the band took worked well with most loyal fans. They appreciated a chance to hear Duran Duran cover some classic songs.

The video for the Reed's "Perfect Day" featured Simon, Nick, John, and Warren, but there was also a surprise guest. Roger Taylor came back to drum for this video and the studio version of "Watching the Detectives." He was actually invited to play on every album since the band's breakup, but he had politely declined each offer.

Roger had the same affinity for some of the songs the band covered, so he decided to help with the album. His work, however, was not used because the entire song was changed, and the drums didn't work with the new version.

Despite this, they were glad to have him back in the studio again. They felt like they were back in the "old days" when they were at the height of their fame. The camera zoomed in on Roger from time to time, but not enough to make his special appearance apparent to those who weren't paying close attention. This, however, was one of his rare appearances until he re-joined the band a few years later. Another guest appearance was made by Terry Bozzio, who played drums for Iggy Pop's "Success."

Unfortunately, Roger's short comeback didn't have much impact on the fans. Some of them who had regained interest after the immediate success of *The Wedding Album* shortly changed their minds after the release of *Thank You*. Simon had the feeling that certain parts of the album were going to be difficult to make.

This brings us back to the song "Ball of Confusion," which was originally recorded by The Temptations. Simon said that he was uncomfortable with the production because he felt under pressure to do a perfect cover version. Of course, perfection cannot be reached, especially in something as subjective as music.

He felt that the only part which really worked for him was the song's chorus. Simon said that he also had a difficult time re-making Sly and the Family Stone's "I Wanna Take You Higher." John and Warren loved the song, so they suggested that it be a part of the album.

They also recorded Neil Young's "Needle and the Damage Done." It wasn't featured on the album, but it was one of the singles. On tour they also covered one of David Bowie's songs, "Rebel Rebel," which was thrown into the new mixture of songs. Another one they wrote while touring Canada was called, "P. L. You."

The latter of the two was mostly performed live, and it never made it onto any of the band's albums. During their live shows, they often encountered a typical reaction from the audience, which consisted of chanting for the early hits, but Duran Duran played their new material, which, at the time, happened to be the cover songs they had reworked. Another one of their popular eighties live performances included a cover of Cockney Rebel's "Make Me Smile (Come Up and See Me)," which was the B-side to "The Reflex."

Despite his success at overcoming his cocaine addiction, John had other personal problems. His stormy marriage with Amanda was struggling. There were various rumours of numerous affairs Amanda had while they were still married.

Things started to fall apart when their daughter, Atlanta, was a year old. Both parents devoted themselves to their child, but with the great success of *The Wedding Album*, Duran Duran began touring again. This was one of the things that upset Amanda. She didn't like it when

John left his family behind, and it put more stress on the relationship. Trying to make family life work was difficult for both.

Also, the fact that John was still using drugs might have played a part in things. The couple tried therapy during the previous year, but their marriage seemed unsalvageable. It was then when the couple decided to separate.

Transitions were occurring in both their lives, and the whole age factor had much to do with their separation. At the time, Amanda was only twenty-three, and John was thirty-five. They both had different friends and lives outside their marriage. Amanda made the claim that she wanted to live her life separate from John so that she could focus most of her attention on Atlanta.

There were also rumours of her being interested in Ashley Hamilton, but she denied them all, stating that they were only friends. Amanda, however, did have an affair with him, and she was also allegedly romantically linked to other celebrities, such as Keanu Reeves and Courtney Love. The latter of the two recorded a cover version of "Hungry Like the Wolf" with her band, Hole.

Meanwhile, Simon extended his talent to another worthy organisation when he performed at a charity event with Luciano Pavarotti. The two of them sang "Ordinary World" together for the War Child Benefit, to provide relief for the children of the war in Bosnia. The performance took place in September 1995 and was a great success. The record was compiled by Pavarotti, and concerts were performed in his hometown of Modena, Italy.

Other celebrities who were a part of the benefit included Meat Loaf, U2, and Michael Bolton. Simon's and U2's performances were the most well-received, and people were absolutely amazed at the quality of sound present in "Ordinary World." The words to the song were sung in both English and Italian during different parts throughout. Pavarotti's and Simon's vocals complimented each other, and the orchestral instruments added more beauty to the song. The event was a great success, and all proceeds from the concerts and the album went to the War Child Benefit.

***

Meanwhile, John moved on to another side project in 1996. He and three other artists, Steve Jones (of The Sex Pistols), Matt Sorum and

Duff McKagan (both of Guns N' Roses) formed a band called Neurotic Outsiders.

It had all started when Sorum called both John and Steve Jones and asked them if they wanted to play some of their songs at an upcoming charity event at the Viper Room Club in Los Angeles.

The band was pleased with the way things were going, and they played shows in L.A. and New York. It was not much later when they were asked to produce an album, which they worked on for most of the rest of the year. John contributed two songs from his first solo album, "Feelings Are Good," and "Always Wrong." The newer versions of these songs went well with Neurotic Outsiders' new album, which gave them an interesting twist.

Although they did record some songs at the Viper Room, with the original album title as *The Story of My Life*, the band decided to record some new songs.

They released their eponymous album in November of that year. The album was produced by Jerry Harrison and they were also surprised when they found out that Madonna signed them to her own label, Maverick Recordings.

Most of the music consisted of heavy metal and hard rock, a different direction from most of John's earlier music. Videos were made for two songs, "Feelings Are Good," and "Jerk."

The music was not classified as punk, and it certainly lacked many elements of pop. By embarking on this technique, John proved that he could successfully work with other mediums of music. Neurotic Outsiders needed a drummer for their band, and John considered asking David Palmer with whom he had worked with before.

David played drums in the video for, "I Don't Want Your Love." He received an offer to join Duran Duran in 1988, but the timing was wrong. This is where Sterling Campbell came into the picture. With all their members established, Neurotic Outsiders were free to continue recording and experimenting with their sound.

While the band had some scattered tours and a certain amount of fame, they were not very well-known, or widely publicised. Another single of theirs, "Seattlehead," was not featured on the album. It was released separately shortly after.

One of the songs off the album, "Better Way" served as a testament to John's new life under clean and sober living. Duff McKagen was the one who convinced the others to record their work. Shortly before,

Neurotic Outsiders played at various clubs, covering Iggy Pop's "I Wanna Be Your Dog" and The Sex Pistols' "Pretty Vacant." They also played shows in New York and Boston alongside Slash and Billy Idol.

At one of the shows, they even covered "Planet Earth." John said part of the band's influence came from the punk rock scene of the late 1970s. They were inspired by bands like the The New York Dolls and The Sex Pistols. Neurotic Outsiders' sound was completely different from what fans of Duran Duran and The Power Station were used to.

By the time autumn rolled around, Neurotic Outsiders started touring America. They performed in various places such as Irving Plaza in New York and Mama Kin in Boston.

John was fond of his new project, and he also liked the fact that he got to sing lead vocals for most of their songs. This way, John got what he wanted because he had an opportunity to portray his true feelings through his words. When Neurotic Outsiders started out in the Viper Room, they had a somewhat casual line-up. Many people joined them on stage, including Simon Le Bon and Billy Idol.

***

Around the same time, The Power Station produced a second album, *Living in Fear*, which was also released in 1996. Bernard Edwards replaced John Taylor on bass guitar. John decided that he didn't want to re-join the band for the making of their second album, even though he considered it in 1991 and again in 1995 (both times the plans fell through).

Unfortunately, Bernard Edwards passed away before the completion of the album. He flew to Japan so he could meet up and perform with Nile Rodgers. Bernard died of a virulent flu in Tokyo, in his sleep, on April 18, 1996. He had quit The Power Station in 1995, shortly before he began work on his first solo album. Some of the most noteworthy songs on the album featured "Living in Fear," "She Can Rock It," "Power Trippin'" and "Fancy That."

Another song, "Charanga," did not make it onto the album, but it was featured on the CD single for "She Can Rock It." Robert Palmer wrote all the words to the song. The album incorporated their old rock and roll sounds with a contemporary edge that attracted both old and new fans. *Living in Fear* was released on the Chrysalis label.

At first, there were varying opinions as to whether or not the album was going to be released in the States. After much debate, it wasn't and American fans had to buy it as an import. Partially due to the fact that *Living in Fear* was not distributed in the United States, not as many fans knew about it. Therefore, it did not reach as large an audience.

When the album began its production, Robert Palmer re-joined to provide vocals. As Duran Duran's fame had diminished since 1985, Robert decided that he would come back to The Power Station.

By that point, Andy was the only Duran Duran member left in The Power Station. The band started to tour again in 1997 to promote their new album. The Power Station's play list included songs from both their albums, Robert Palmer's solo work, and covers of three James Brown songs, "Hot Pants," "Rufus," and "Tell Me Something Good."

The tours were well-received in the States. Some fans were eager to attend the shows, which sustained interest in the tour, but the attendances didn't match that of the 1985 tours, especially because The Power Station's fame was parallel to that of Duran Duran. Despite a valiant effort, this more or less meant the end of the line for The Power Station. Their "comeback" tour had not done as well as anticipated.

In 1996, Andy and Simon ran into each other in Tokyo while Andy was touring with The Power Station. The two had not spoken for years, but it didn't take long for them to contemplate a reunion. John and Andy talked about the idea while Andy was working on *Living in Fear*.

Certain parts of the idea seemed unrealistic and undecided. Besides the obvious question of band dynamics, they also had to ask themselves if they could regain the loyalty and interest of their fans.

John and Andy were busy with their own side projects, while Simon was thinking of another Duran Duran album. It appeared that the guys had a lot to think about before reconvening to start something new.

Reach Up For The Sunrise

CHAPTER 10

Another Taylor Takes Leave

John Taylor left the band in early 1997. He thought over his decision and decided that he needed room to expand his horizons. Part of the reason for his decision was because he was tired of commuting back and forth between the United States and England to the band's London office. He had just recently gained dual citizenship. While John felt he was making the right decision, he dreaded having to make the phone calls to Simon, Nick, and Warren.

The course of his life was changing, and he wanted to spend more time with his new family. Although John originally "left" the band in 1995, he made his official announcement on January 18, 1997. As a last hurrah for fans, he thought of having a reunion tour with the Fab Five line-up and Warren Cuccurullo.

When he suggested the idea to Andy, the former lead guitarist said he wouldn't participate in such an event, contrary to his previous statement. John personally relayed to Simon, Nick, Roger and Warren what Andy had said. That was the easy part. The hard part entailed telling the fans what was decided in the end.

The news came as a shock and a blow to the fans. Many of them didn't know how to express what they felt about what the band had decided. Even though they had over ten years to cope with Andy and Roger leaving the band, many fans still found it hard to accept this news.

Many were shocked as the news was reported by the press. Fans posted their distraught responses to various threads on the Internet, and some had even tried to contact John personally to share their disappointment.

Some placed the blame on Warren, claiming that he urged John to quit the band, which was not the case at all. John's solo career had started to take off, and he wanted to further experiment with his new material. Nick said that John's reason for leaving the band was due to the fact that he purchased a home with a recording studio in L.A. and John wanted to remain there.

In addition to his house and recording studio, John also owned a record label. He felt that the strain of travelling back and forth, to and from England, would wear him down too much. John wanted to focus on his solo career, which saw its beginnings in 1986. The founding father of Duran Duran was gone shortly after the band started work on their 1997 album.

Medazzaland reached stores in the United States on October 14, 1997. The most popular single from the album was "Electric Barbarella." The song's title was a tribute to the band's namesake. The video features Sara Stockbridge, a British model, who plays the part of a cyber-sex doll for the amusement of the band members. Stockbridge resembles Jane Fonda's character in the movie *Barbarella*. This electric Barbarella was purchased to keep the band company, although they get more than they bargained for when she short-circuits and loses control.

They achieved another feat when they became the first band to legally sell their single on the Internet. Fans purchased copies of "Electric Barbarella" online via Liquid Audio. Because of this, many record stores in America refused to sell Duran Duran's music at the time. They felt threatened by new technology and the direction in which the music industry was headed.

The CD version of *Medazzaland* included the hit single, and various remixes of the song, such as the "Tee's Club Mix," and the "All Fired Up Mix." The director's cut of the video could be played on computer. The other single from *Medazzaland*, "Out of My Mind," was included as a part of the soundtrack for the movie *The Saint*, starring Val Kilmer. This was the third song Simon had written for his departed friend, David Miles. "Out of My Mind" also has a video. It features the band members being portrayed as ghosts and Simon dressing as an old man.

When John left, Simon pondered the loss and claimed that he wouldn't get sentimental about the situation. Although the remaining members of the band worried about their success following the departure of their founder, they enjoyed the fact that they got to experiment with their sound. The further incorporation of electronics in their music allowed them to add in their own drums and bass sounds even though *Medazzaland* wasn't intended to be solely classified as an electronic work.

Simon stated that he was glad the band took longer on the production of the album and to put more thought into their work. Since *Thank You* failed to generate very much success, they knew they had to do better on their next album. This served as a goal and helped them focus on a more positive outcome.

Even though John left the band during the beginning phases of *Medazzaland*, he was still being interviewed for various magazines. In one article, he made the statement that Duran Duran came out of the punk era. They wanted to experiment with any artistic sound that came from their instruments. Their tenth studio album was an experiment within itself, and it seemed to pertain more to the interests of the younger generation.

Medazzaland contained strong elements of techno music, which was growing in popularity. Although his name was not included in the liner notes, one can hear John's voice on a few of the songs. *Medazzaland* was an album that helped Duran Duran redefine some of their success, and it provided its listeners with a new sound that resembled alternative rock. During the early 2000s, there were even conversation candy hearts which read, *"BE MY ICON"* which many fans thought of as tribute to Duran Duran.

Simon claimed to have come up with the name for the album while he was undergoing dental surgery. The doctor hooked him up to an IV and fed him a drug called Midazolam. He also stated that he was conscious during the surgery, but his memory of most of the event was gone.

When Nick and Warren noticed that he was still in a weird state, they made a remark to him that he was "still in medazzaland." Some members of the band had also experimented with a psychedelic drug called 3,4-Methylenedioxyamphetamine, or MDA for short.

Nick lent his lyrical and vocal talents to the album because Simon was contributing less material for a little over a year. *Medazzaland's* title track was originally intended to be an instrumental, but Nick was responsible for providing the vocals. He said that he was motivated by the idea of paranoia to the extreme.

When Simon heard Nick's vocals on the track, he was really impressed with his skill and the fact that his voice was going to be heard on the album. Simon still suffered from writer's block, however, and was not contributing much to the new album.

According to Nick, Simon was going through a difficult time. He felt very isolated. Yasmin could sense that something was wrong with her husband. She came to the conclusion that Simon was not putting his heart and soul into the music because he was still perplexed by John's departure. Simon made the claim that he would not be the same without him. Even though it was hard for him, Simon worked with the band during his bout of depression.

Some fans said that Duran Duran's new sound took a lot of getting used to, but it finally settled in and was embraced by those who learned to appreciate the album. Although *Medazzaland* did not receive as much acclaim as *The Wedding Album*, it still fared better than *Thank You*.

After the release of the new album, loyal fans found themselves formed in a line at a Virgin Megastore. They gathered up all their items from the 1980s and patiently waited for autographs. These fans wanted to prove that Duran Duran had the staying power, which helped them live up to their name. The band had just released their tenth studio album.

Even during the late eighties, Duran Duran's fame was still compared to that of The Beatles. They created such a phenomenon that would not disappear so easily. Shortly after the release of *Medazzaland*, Duran Duran had sold a total of over twenty million records worldwide. Then, more than ever, their most faithful fans expressed their complete adoration.

Nick admitted that Duran Duran aimed some of their new work toward people who were already in their twenties, although some younger people liked it as well. They thought it was a good move on their part since it appeared that lesser-known bands from the 1980s had a difficult time getting anyone under the age of thirty to listen to their music.

Ever since the days of *Rio*, younger female fans seemed to be the key demographic for Duran Duran's fan base. It seemed that things were finally changing for the band in that respect, and Nick was pleased with the recent shift.

Medazzaland is known for its interesting cover art. An artist by the name of Andrew Day was responsible for creating the paintings for the album. Duran Duran originally wanted to have a photograph taken by Andrew featured on the cover, but they stuck with the finished results of the paintings because they came out so much better. Simon professed to have discovered Andrew at an art college in London.

He introduced him to Nick and Warren as they viewed his creations. They were impressed with what they saw, especially Warren, who recruited Andrew to produce more artwork for his solo albums. Warren was also impressed with the fact that Andrew succeeded under pressure since this was his first corporate project. He is also said to have done some more creative work for Warren's website.

The album's melancholy, yet insightful tracks helped the band reach a slightly younger audience. One song, "Michael You've Got a Lot to Answer for," expresses Simon Le Bon's sorrow over the death of another close friend, Michael Hutchence — lead singer of INXS, who committed suicide.

Some people hold to the theory that he accidentally asphyxiated himself while trying to enhance his pleasure in a sexual act. In an interview, Simon said he and Michael were best friends at the time of his death. One could tell that the news shattered Simon.

Through the song, many fans knew what Simon was going through during this time of loss. It was a sad time, indeed, for Michael's survivors. Although the song is nowhere near as well-known as many other Duran Duran tunes, fans can draw a parallel between "Michael You've Got a Lot to Answer for," "Out of My Mind," "Ordinary World," and "Do You Believe in Shame?" because Simon expressed his sorrow, in all four songs, over the loss of dear friends.

During this time, Nick and Simon worked together on writing and producing two new songs, "Pop Trash Movie" and "Studio 54." The latter of the two was produced for the long-awaited Blondie compilation, which was scrapped right before its completion.

A tribute album, known simply as *The Duran Duran Tribute Album*, featured bands which were popular at the time, such as Goldfinger, Reel Big Fish, The Deftones, and Eve's Plumb covering their hit songs. It was released by Mojo Records on October 7, 1997. A tribute concert followed shortly after on the 12th. A few of the aforementioned bands paid tribute, citing Duran Duran as their favourite band and source of inspiration.

The main sound of the album consisted of alternative rock and ska, which gave a new twist to fifteen of Duran Duran's most famous works. There were, however, some who felt that the band may have not been ready for a tribute album, including some of the band members themselves.

Nick Rhodes felt that tribute albums were usually dedicated to bands whose career had already ended. Duran Duran made the point that the band was still making records and were nowhere ready to give up on what they had started all those years ago.

****

John was doing well in his solo career, but his love life was in turmoil. This was when he and Amanda officially got divorced. The couple originally separated in 1995, but the separation became a divorce once everything was finalised. Although they remain in contact for the sake of Atlanta, John and Amanda moved on and went their separate ways.

John's first album, *Feelings Are Good*, also came out in stores this year. The album was first released on the Internet in 1995 and manufactured by B5 Records. Two songs from Neurotic Outsiders' album, "Feelings Are Good" and "Always Wrong" were featured on John's first solo work.

The album also consisted of other songs that John wrote when he was suffering from problems in his marriage. "Losing You" was a sad ballad about his marital struggles with Amanda. John deeply expresses his sorrow over losing the woman he loved. A hidden track on the CD is a song called "Full Moon Over Atlanta," which is dedicated to his daughter.

Since then, John has produced many other albums, as well as a live 6-track EP *Terroristen* (1998), now out of print and difficult to find.

John had been friends with musicians Gerry Rafferty and John Amato for years, but he just started working with them on the production of his second album. John and his band were very excited to have their first show outside of California, and he said it was a good feeling to be touring again while promoting his work.

Some of John's other solo albums include: *Meltdown* (1998), *Live Cuts* (1999), *The Japan Album* (1999), *MetaFour* (2002), *Techno for Two* (1999), *Retreat into Art* (2001), and *Resume* (1985-86). *Resume* consisted of early songs he produced with Jonathan Ellias. A sampler CD was also made. It went along with the purchase of the magazine, *JT Retro*, manufactured by his official website.

Retreat into Art was released as a compilation of songs from his

Another Taylor Takes Leave

other albums. It was a limited edition. Only 999 copies were made, and the album was only available through John's official website. (I was lucky enough to receive copy No. 900.)

John was always fond of the performing arts, and he decided to further expand his career by giving acting a try. John played various parts in movies, such as *Sugartown* (1999), *Drowning on Dry Land* (1999), *Four Dogs Playing Poker* (2000), *Vegas, City of Dreams* (2001), and *She-Bat* (2001). Most of these were independent films which did not receive much acclaim.

John also had a small role in the 2000 Flintstones movie *Viva Rock Vegas* as a famous rock star. John recoils as he remembers the character he played, Keith Rich-Rock. The whole account, to him, was a bad experience.

John also played various roles on television. In 1985, he played the part of a computer hacker in the series, *Timeslip*. John brought his TV acting skills into the mainstream in December 2000 when he played the Ghost of Christmas Present in the VH1 original movie *A Diva's Christmas Carol*, starring Vanessa Williams.

He also starred in a 2001 VH1 original mini-series called *Strange Frequencies*. His character, Jimmy Blitz, was a handsome, but egotistical rock star, who had a propensity to trash hotel rooms. John was also featured on a 2002 episode of *That '80s Show* as a character named Zeke.

Reach Up For The Sunrise

CHAPTER 11

And Then There Were Three

From late 1997 to May 2001, the line-up consisted of Simon Le Bon, Nick Rhodes, and Warren Cuccurullo. Nick was the only founding member left in the band. This may have been one of the reasons why Duran Duran did not have very much publicity during the time.

In 1998, Capitol Records made an effort to recapture the interest of the wayward fans. A compilation album, *Greatest*, was released combining the hits from the first album, *Duran Duran* through to *Medazzaland*. *Greatest* was also made into a video to go along with the album. Although, just as was the case with *Arena*, there was some song variation between the CD and the video.

Later in the year, Nick expressed his exasperation at people who associated the band with only their eighties material. Duran Duran had so many accomplishments since then, and 1993's *The Wedding Album* was probably the best example to prove the point.

Nick also felt that Duran Duran's best work came out of the nineties. He added that nostalgia was nothing with which the band should be associated. While one can understand much of the general public's lack of knowledge concerning the band, it is exasperating to think that people have not even heard of their more recent successes.

Some are completely unaware that the band is still around, making music, touring and expanding their horizons. Duran Duran survived and thrived from the 1980s, and for this reason, they are most deserving of their well-earned success. They also toured in England then went to the United States the following year

Another compilation album released in 1998 was *The Essential Duran Duran: Night Mixes*. The physical CD album includes a cardboard case with a regular jewel case inside. The liner note booklet contains a well-written foreword by Nick. The music includes twelve remixed tracks which were hit songs from 1981 to 1985. There was also a bonus CD in the back flap of the cardboard case. That CD contained the "New Moon on Monday (Extended Mix)," which could be run and played on computer.

The following year, another compilation album was released, *Strange Behaviour*. The album shares its name with their '87 tour, even though it contained no live performances. The first CD contains many of the same remixed songs from *The Essential Duran Duran: Night Mixes* album, but the second CD includes hits from *Notorious*, to *The Wedding Album*. The band also made more public appearances on television and was featured on VH1's *Behind the Music* and *Hard Rock Live*, which was aired early in 2000.

John suffered a personal loss in 1998 when his mother, Jean, passed away from leukaemia. She was seventy-seven years old. Her illness was very short-term, as it only lasted for a few weeks. The doctors did what they could to ease the pain by giving her more morphine, but it was all to no avail.

John was deeply saddened by the loss because he and his mother were very close. As expected, Jack was also very shaken by his wife's death. After John wrote a song about her death, "The Only One," he finally felt some closure and appreciated that she lived a long and happy life.

Right around this time, Nick and his long-time girlfriend, Madeline Farley, parted ways. Their breakup was emotionally difficult, and it ended badly. Nick was heartbroken when Madeline left him. He knew he would take a long time to recover because of how much he loved her.

All was not lost in love, however, because John found someone with whom he felt he had a lot in common. In 1999, John had married his sweetheart, Gela Nash. John had proposed to Gela on Christmas Eve 1998, the same night that he married Amanda seven years earlier. John and Gela had a civil ceremony in Los Vegas on March 27, 1999. The wedding only had three witnesses. Gela's sister, John's daughter, and Gela's son.

The couple met at a party thrown by one of their mutual friends, Nancy. When John met Gela, he was instantly smitten, and he knew that he had to find out who she was. Of course, Gela didn't really know who John was either because she didn't seem to know too much about music. In his autobiography, John joked that Gela knew so little about rock music she thought every song she'd heard on the radio was by Genesis.

Like John, Gela had been previously married. She had two children, Travis and Zoe, with her first husband. John felt an immediate bond with his stepchildren, and that was one of the reasons why he decided to quit Duran Duran. He wanted the five of them to become a close-knit family.

Gela, along with her partner, Pamela Skaist-Levy, formed the successful clothing label, Juicy Couture, in 1996. The new clothing line swept the world by storm and was especially popular among the Hollywood set.

The successful pair of designers had numerous articles printed in magazines, such as *People*, in which many celebrities endorsed their products. John, along with Pamela's husband, Jefery Levy, gave the two designers their input when they created their first line of men's clothing in December 2003. Fans of Juicy Couture, as well as Duranies, were eager to purchase their products.

Nick also had a chance to begin an "acting career" when he had a small voice part as a Canadian bomber pilot in the 1999 *South Park* movie *Bigger, Louder, and Uncut*. Nick was good friends with Trey Parker, one of the creators of the show.

Trey, reportedly, was also a fan of Duran Duran's music. The creators of *South Park* made another reference to Duran Duran for one of their Christmas episodes. Santa sang part of "Rio" at a lounge club because, according to him, there were not enough Christmas songs about Santa. Nick's fondness for animation made him a good candidate for the movie, even though his part was very small. Another one of Nick's favourite shows is *The Simpsons*. He has been a fan of the animated sitcom for years.

Shortly after *Greatest* was released they split with Capitol/EMI in 1998. The guys felt that it was time for a change, and they were initially glad that they moved on to a different company when they signed to Hollywood Records, whose parent company was the Walt Disney Company. Nick felt that the intimacy of this new partnership would benefit Duran Duran more when it came to their musical needs.

The Walt Disney Company was confident about their ability to support the band because they felt it would be mutually advantageous for both parties.

In 2000, Duran Duran released their last album as a trio, *Pop*

Trash. It was available for purchase in the United States on June 13, 2000. Their *Pop Trash* tour kicked off about a month later. Before the band produced the album, there were interview rumours that the album was going to be called "Hallucinating Elvis."

They had other record labels release *Pop Trash* in different countries. Universal released the album in Canada. *Pop Trash* was also released by Avex in Japan, Edel in Europe, and Festival in Australia and New Zealand. The band also went under their own management under the names of TV Mania, and SYN Productions. TV Mania was created by Nick and Warren, and SYN Productions was Simon's production company.

The songs from the new album were published by Private Parts and Skin Trade Music. During this time, there was also a lot of cynicism in England about the band experimenting with their sound. Duran Duran, however, shrugged it off and claimed that it was a process which every artist eventually underwent. Members of the band also noted that the same thing happened after the release of 1990's *Liberty*.

While the album cover looked promising, containing a photograph of Liberace's silver car in contrast with a black background, the music did not live up the expectations of some fans.

The band's first single, "Someone Else, Not Me," was released worldwide on May 2, 2000. The song was recorded in three languages, English, French, and Spanish. It was originally intended for both the Spanish and French versions of "Someone Else Not Me" to be included as bonus tracks on *Pop Trash*.

Warren also had a lot of input on the album as he did with *Liberty*, and his influence was known. The song Simon and Nick wrote in 1997, "Pop Trash Movie," was inspired by Andy Warhol. When Duran Duran performed in Pittsburgh for the *Pop Trash* Tour, Simon told the audience they were going to play the song as part of the encore since Andy Warhol was from the city.

Due to further experimentation, Simon wrote songs that sounded like his solo works for the album. The most Beatle-esque song, "Starting to Remember," was written by Warren after his father's death.

Alternately, another track, "The Sun Doesn't Shine Forever," was written by Nick about his rough breakup with Madeline. *Pop Trash* was musical and lyrical experimentation which brought the band's work to a different level. After all, musical change contributed to their great success in the early eighties.

Although Duran Duran put forth a good effort, the album was not very successful, and sales were lower than anticipated. Even though the band had a following of devoted fans, they still lacked interest from the general public. The slightest change in detail was not as exciting as it was during the height of their fame. The public is fickle when it comes to entertainment. It seems that the media seems to build up stars only to tear them down as soon as their fame wanes. The music industry is a competitive dog-eat-dog business.

The concerts from the *Pop Trash* Tour consisted mainly of dedicated fans and those who were eager for the band to play their hits. When they started to play their classics like "Save a Prayer" and "Hungry Like the Wolf," they received thunderous applause, but when they delved into the songs from *Pop Trash*, the most they got were random cheers and polite applause from the audience. As is the case with many groups, the fans seemed like they only wanted to hear the hits and anticipated little patience for newer and less familiar material.

Some items sold at the concerts included postcards of Simon, Nick, and Warren and other designs featuring *Pop Trash* themes. The photographs were taken by Andrew Day, who designed the paintings for their previous album. Those postcards were just among a few things that fans could purchase at the shows.

If one took the opportunity to scan the audience at one of these shows, he or she could easily make the observation that many in attendance were in their thirties or forties. While most fans may have attended the shows in hopes of hearing Duran Duran's greatest hits, some of them found they could relate to the new music from *Pop Trash*. This is a good example of how their music matured with the fans. That's not to say that Duran Duran's music has lost any meaning, rather, it seemed to create something new for those who underwent the change in time.

The band had two additional members who joined them for the *Pop Trash* Tour, Joe Travers on drums and Wes Wehmiller on bass. Even though some fans acknowledged their efforts, Joe and Wes were not quite like John and Roger, whose posters dominated the walls of their teenage fans.

As many have known since the eighties, Duran Duran was no strangers to making cutting edge videos. Their first computer animated video was made for the song "Someone Else, Not Me," and it was shown for some time on VH1. This video, like most of their others, can be viewed on YouTube.

The Internet became prominent in the nineties and could have assisted the band nearly as much as the advent of MTV the previous decade. As mentioned before, Duran Duran was the first band to sell their single on the Internet. They also had a lot of Internet promotion for *Pop Trash*.

Hollywood Records worked with several websites to promote the album, such as ARTISTdirect, Sonic Net, Launch, Spin Online, MTV.com, and VH1.com. Since no one was really sure how much airplay Duran Duran's music would receive, it was important that Hollywood Records advertised and promoted the new album online. *Pop Trash*, just as the single, "Electric Barbarella," was sold through Duran Duran's official website.

In 1999, while the band was touring in the United States, fans had the option of voting for their new favourite songs. Many of the votes were placed for "Someone Else Not Me," which was one of the things that prompted the band to release it as their first single.

A great deal of information is provided on the band on their official website and community fan site. The Internet provides a place for Duranies to come together in cyberspace so they can share stories, music, and pictures with one another. Numerous web pages were created for the band and its individual members.

Duran Duran also has an official fan club and fan boards, where people can post and converse online. The band didn't take long to express their fondness for the Internet and it helped them in various ways.

John Taylor was one of the first band members to make the Internet work for him because he was able to advertise his new albums and converse with co-workers and some of his fans. Some may argue that the Internet hurt the band's record sales because of music file sharing programs, but others disagree.

Online sales have increased Duran Duran's album sales, and file sharing programs allow fans to have access to rare and out-of-print material. Also, many Duranies find that the Internet has worked to their advantage.

However during this period they soon became disillusioned with their new label and wanted to get out of the contract. According to Simon, Hollywood Records dropped the album almost as quickly as they picked it up.

CHAPTER 12

The Strongest Comeback!

In May 2001, Duran Duran officially announced that they had reunited the classic line-up. Fans who had waited fifteen years for this news were excited that their wish had finally been fulfilled.

In lieu of Duran Duran's recent success, Capitol Records re-released the band's biggest selling album to date, *Rio*. The album came out in stores on July 3, 2001, in a jewel case with a limited-edition design. It also includes videos for three of the band's most successful singles off the album "Rio," "Hungry Like the Wolf," and "Save a Prayer."

Even though they were no longer with Capitol Records, the company retained the back catalogue from the most successful period. Capitol Records also knew the reunion would be to their advantage and increase sales for the label. As a result, many fans purchased the re-released version of *Rio* with their renewed interest in the band.

The whole idea for the reunion started while John was vacationing in Hawaii in 2000. He ran into the band's old lawyer, with whom he discussed the possibility of a comeback. John called Nick and Simon the next day, and the two of them liked the idea of getting back together.

Another thing that sparked the reunion was when John and Gela ran into Simon, drinking coffee at Barney's restaurant in Beverly Hills. Duran Duran was in town, playing shows to promote *Pop Trash*. Gela invited Simon to their house and spend some time with them. Since Gela wasn't going to take "no" for an answer, it was a date. Thus, this chain of events got the ball rolling, and everything just seemed to fall into place soon after that.

The other two Taylors, however, were not as eager as the other three. Roger agreed to come back, but for a while, he was hesitant to re-join. It was not long after when Andy admitted that he would not have re-joined the band if Roger declined the offer. John felt another alternate version of the band would not have worked.

The five individuals first had to see if they could still be in the same room and get along together before they began to work on anything. During May 2001, The Fab Five were back in the rehearsal studio for the first time in years.

News of the reunion came a surprise to Warren Cuccurullo when a special delivery letter arrived at his house. The letter stated that he was no longer a member of Duran Duran. Warren, was especially aggrieved since he put so much time and effort into the band. He was also hurt that his band mates didn't tell him in person.

Duran Duran's manager informed Warren that the other band members were afraid of what his reaction to the letter was going to be. That is why they chose to notify him by post. Although this meant the end of his career with Duran Duran, Warren maintained that he would remain friends with Nick and Simon. Fans had many mixed opinions about Warren leaving the band. Many were sad to see him go, while others were happy that The Fab Five were reunited.

Warren, Simon, and Nick still played their scheduled dates in Japan. The three dates listed were as follows: June 16th at the Tokyo International Forum, June 19th at Shibuya-ax in Tokyo, and June 22nd in Koseinenkin, Osaka, Japan. The fans who attended those three shows were the last ones to see the band perform as a trio. Warren wished the band good luck with their reunion and said he hoped it would bring them a lot of success.

While the band was certainly eager to get back into the saddle, John was extremely nervous during the night before their first show took place. It had been a long time since Duran Duran was back in the limelight, and he didn't quite know what to think. Instead of folding under the pressure, however, John called on a higher power. He prayed to God so that he would overcome his fears. And surely enough, it worked. God had answered John's prayers and he performed successfully on stage in front of his fans.

****

Since Warren was no longer in Duran Duran, he revaluated his options, which led him to decide that to team up again with Dale Bozzio. The two performed some shows on the West Coast of the U.S. in 2003. They were also joined by Wes Wehmiller and Joe Travers.

The Strongest Comeback!

Warren had a lot of new ideas that he used in his songs. He also released several solo albums both before and after he left Duran Duran. These include; *Thanks 2 Frank* (1995), *Machine Language* (1997), *Roadrage*, (on which he performed an instrumental version of "Ordinary World") (1998), *The Blue* (featuring Shankar on vocals) (2000), *Trance Formed* (2003), *Playing in Tongues* (2009), *Chicanery* (2010) *The Master* (2014), *'N Liten Up* (2015), and *Missing Person* (2019). *Chicanery* was a collaboration between Warren Cuccurullo and Neil Carlill.

Even though Warren was very close to Mayko, he and Claudia, have since split. The couple met during Duran Duran's 88/89 tour. He dated a woman by the name of Donna Nguyen for a long while.

In 2002, Warren purchased an Italian restaurant in Santa Monica, California, called Via Veneto. The restaurant is a favourite with celebrities who live in the area.

Another album which Warren recorded was called *'N Liten Up*, a concept album. For many years, fans thought the album was never going to be released, but it finally came out in 2015. Warren self-released the album via Bandcamp. He worked with many familiar artists for the album, including Dale Bozzio, who provides a spoken voice role. Two of the songs off the album were written by Nick Rhodes.

In 2003 Warren was hospitalised. He is always the type to put his health first, especially since he does not smoke or do drugs. The concept for *'N Liten Up* was inspired by a spiritual epiphany he had after surviving the illness. The album guides its listeners through his newfound view on life by use of different forms of music. Parts of the story unfold as it is told by different characters.

****

Now that Duran Duran was back together, they needed to start working on new material. In 2002, the band started collaborating on their ideas for the new album. One of the first songs they started writing was called "Nice." Many other songs were written during this time as they began to practice and experiment with their new music.

Elsewhere Nick Rhodes and Stephen Duffy regrouped in 2001 and started a little side project. They called their band The Devils. Nick and Steve recorded the songs they wrote during their early days at Bates' Toy Corner.

In 2000, Stephen came across one of the old demo tapes he made with the earliest line-up of Duran Duran. He ran into Nick a little while later at a fashion show, and the two began to talk about their old music. Nick and Steve decided to relive their early days by recording some of these songs onto an album.

The Devils' album, entitled *Dark Circles*, was released in July 2002. One song, "Hawks Do Not Share" was one that Nick and Steve experimented with back in the earliest days of Duran Duran. The song's title was inspired by a quote from Ernest Hemingway's *A Moveable Feast*, which is a series of memoirs talking about the author's years in Paris.

Nick and Steve were excited that it was finally going to be released on an album, nearly twenty-five years later. One track that may strike a sentimental chord is entitled "Barbarellas." In it, Steve sang about when they played their first gigs. Through the songs, many fans could imagine what it was like during Duran Duran's early days at the club.

While The Devils made a video for their song, "Big Store," and played some tours, they did not follow with any other collaborations, so the project was very short-lived.

Nick may not have known it at the time, but he was soon to meet another woman, Meredith Ostrom, through the hands of fate. Nick might not have left a good first impression on Meredith, but she is still able to look back at their first meeting and laugh. The two of them were on the corner of the street, waiting for a taxi.

Meredith thought he was rude because Nick didn't offer the cab to her when it came. Since they hailed the same car, she thought he should not make her wait. The two compromised and agreed to share the cab.

Meredith felt it was a brush of fate that had brought them together. She was only in England for two days when she met Nick. Coincidentally, they were heading for the same place without knowing it, a party for Mario Testino, celebrating the recent publication of his third book, *Alive*.

Meredith soon started talking to Nick, thus getting to know him better. She was surprised to find that he was the famous keyboard player for Duran Duran because she didn't recognise him or even know his name. Nick and Meredith didn't take long after that to grow fond of each other, and they started dating shortly after they met.

Sadly, the relationship came to an end in February 2009. Since their breakup, Meredith has been linked with Topper Mortimer. Even though they've been apart for years, Nick and Meredith still remain friends.

Meredith also played parts in various movies and made appearances on television shows. Some films and TV shows in which she made appearances include; *Taxi Bhaiya* (1996), *Love Goggles* (1999), *Sex and the City* (2000), *'R Xmas* (2001), *My Name Is Tanino* (2002), *Love Actually* (for which she had a bit part as one of the girls in the "mock Robert Palmer" Christmas music video) (2003), *When Will I Be Loved* (2004), *The Great New Wonderful* (2005), *Bizarre Love Triangle* (2005), Played (2006), *Factory Girl* (2006), *Feel the Noise* (2007), *Once a Garden* (2008), *Nine Miles Down* (2009), *Boogie Woogie* (2009), *The Heavy* (2010), *The Prelude* (2010), *Moving Target* (2011), *The Ninth Cloud* (2012), *Magic City* (2013), and Barcelona Baby! (2017).

For a few years in between the band's comeback and the release of their latest album, they had trouble finding a record label. Duran Duran left Hollywood Records shortly after the release of *Pop Trash*. The Fab Five reunited and they financed the album without assistance from a record label. Eventually, they signed back with EMI Records.

In 2003, rumours of a Duran Duran CD box began formulating. It was said to have contained all the band's big hits from 1981-1985. These rumours became the truth when the box set, *Singles 1981-1985*, was released in April 2003, and it included everything that was promised. Even though the box set did not contain biographical information on the band, many fans were still anxious to purchase it.

Included in the front is a folding picture of the band, taken in 1981. Each of the thirteen CD cases contained the original artwork, which was designed for the singles when they were produced on record. Some bonus songs included many of their early B-sides, such as "Khanada," (Simon wrote this song for a girl he liked) "Faster Than Light," "Like an Angel" and, of course, "Late Bar." There was also a live performance of their song "(I'm Looking for) Cracks in the Pavement" from *Seven and the Ragged Tiger*.

During the summer of 2003, news of the reunion spread nationwide. Original fans dug out their old records, magazines, and photo albums and listened to their music like they were fifteen again.

Durandamonium nearly approached the level it was at during 1983. When the band kicked off their reunion tour in Japan, Japanese fans felt and acted just like it was the early eighties all over again. Excited fans sang the words of their favourite songs to each other. Some ran down the hallway, hoping for a chance to catch a closer glimpse of or possibly meet the band members who defined their youth.

They played their new hits and had the same amount of energy on the stage as they did in their earlier days. Hit songs included a wide range of their music from their entire career, such as "Ordinary World," "A View to a Kill," and "Hungry Like the Wolf." They performed "White Lines" from their album *Thank You*. Another new song that was played for the crowds was "Virus," which was intended to be included on the new album but never made the cut.

People in the United States were just as excited to see the reunion. During the middle of 2003, Duran Duran were featured in many different magazines and appeared on television shows. Celebrity fans, such as Christina Applegate and Jennifer Anniston, showed their excitement for the band and their music all over again. While some thought of the whole thing as a nostalgia trip, dedicated fans knew that it was going to amount to much more than that. Most of the 2003 reunion tour was sold out. These were the band's first performances together since Live Aid in 1985.

They weren't hesitant to admit that their 2001 comeback was spurred by eighties nostalgia. Roger Taylor, in one interview, was quick to express his views on the matter. He said that Duran Duran regained their fan base due to the fact that eighties nostalgia had made its way into the 21st century. And some say that we are still experiencing eighties nostalgia today.

While in Southern France writing new material, they had the opportunity to work with other well-known performers, such as Alicia Keyes, Mary J. Blige, Beyoncé Knowles, Usher, Good Charlotte, Pearl Jam, and Lincoln Park.

Further experimentation of their sound included the incorporation of alternative rock and R&B. These formats were very popular genres of music, and the band felt that their new sound was going to work for them.

During the summer of 2003, Simon and Nick worked with a band called The Dandy Warhols. The two of them provided instruments and vocals for The Dandy Warhols' new album *Welcome to the Monkey House*. Simon and Nick sang back-up vocals for a song called "Plan A." Works from The Dandy Warhols' previous albums appeared on the movie soundtracks for *Good Will Hunting* and *There's Something About Mary*.

During September of the same year, they made a special appearance on MTV. They were awarded a Lifetime Achievement Award at the *MTV Video Music Awards* in New York. Warren, although no longer a part of the band, received one as well. The award was presented by Kelly Osborne and Avril Lavine.

Upon seeing the statues set up on the table, John made a joke that no one in the band should walk off the stage without holding one of them in their arms. The crowd went wild, and Duranies everywhere rejoiced. Nick also joked that Duran Duran had just been *Punk'd*. Although their reactions were a little subdued at the time, they were glad to be the only recipients of this prestigious award.

This was certainly a step up for the band since the 1990 *MTV Music Award* show, for which they couldn't even get tickets. Soon after, at the BRIT Awards, they were presented with an award that recognised them for their Outstanding Contribution to Music.

More excitement was generated when they played several stadium shows in Australia and New Zealand during the fall of 2003. They were the opening act for former Take That singer Robbie Williams. Even though they weren't the main headliner, many fans attended these concerts in order to see their favourite band onstage again.

While things were looking up for the band in 2003, they also suffered two losses. Both Robert Palmer and Tony Thompson passed away.

On September 26, 2003, Robert suffered a heart attack at the age of 54. He died at the Warwick Hotel after a dinner and a movie with his long-time girlfriend, Mary Ambrose. Because Robert was said to be in good health nearly two weeks before, his death was a big shock to everyone. Robert was living in Lugano, Switzerland at the time of his death. He is survived by Mary, his parents, and his two children, Jim and Jane. His funeral was held in Switzerland the following week.

Robert was born in Yorkshire, but was raised in Malta, where his father was stationed. He went back to the United Kingdom not long after he reached his teens. It was then when he gained an interest in music. Robert was involved with various bands, including Vinegar Joe in the early seventies, alongside Elkie Brooks, which nudged him into early fame.

When the band broke up in 1974, he headed over to the United

States to get a start on his solo career. He teamed up with funk fusion band Meters and Lowell George of Little Feat fame to record his first single "Sneakin' Sally Through the Alley."

The song that brought him the most acclaim during his solo career was "Addicted to Love" from the album *Riptide*. On October 2, 2003, shortly after the death of Robert Palmer, Duran Duran attended the *Q Magazine* Awards in Park Lane Hotel in London. The band won yet another Lifetime Achievement Award, which was presented by Nile Rodgers. Still saddened by their recent loss, they dedicated the award to the memory of Robert.

Tony Thompson died on November 12, 2003 from renal cell cancer, a mere three days before his forty-ninth birthday. He was born in New York City on November 15, 1954.

Tony had minimal success after starting his musical career, but things started to take off when he joined the seventies soul group, Chic. They are best known for their No.1 hit, "Le Freak," from 1978. Tony's rising reputation and talent enabled him to get work with many famous performers, such as Diana Ross, David Bowie, Madonna, and Mick Jagger.

In 1985, Tony received a phone call that he thought would change his life. Tony was invited to play drums for Led Zeppelin at Live Aid, an offer which he gladly accepted. Shortly after, he started to record new material with them. Tony, however, was involved in a serious car accident, which forced him to delay his work. Unfortunately, the music he recorded with Led Zeppelin was never released.

Tony's death was especially hard on the members of Duran Duran because they had to perform a show in Cleveland the next day. Although they deeply missed their friend, The Fab Five remained strong and professional, thus enabling them to put on a great performance.

Tony is survived by his wife, Patrice, and their two children. A benefit concert was held for him on December 16 at the Hard Rock Café in Los Angeles. Although Tony Thompson and Robert Palmer are gone, their memory will live on through their music, in the minds of the fans who've cherished them over the years.

There was also some added excitement for football fans on Super Bowl Sunday for Super Bowl XXXVIII (the Carolina Rams vs. the New England Patriots) Duran Duran performed their 1984 hit, "The Wild Boys," at the private tailgate party. The performance was aired on CBS a few hours before the kick-off.

The Strongest Comeback!

In April 2004, Roger and Giovanna ended their close to twenty-year marriage. While the two of them enjoyed a faithful and loving marriage, their differences put a rift between them. Giovanna was unhappy that Roger re-joined Duran Duran. Since they were married for many years during which Roger was not in the band, the couple enjoyed a quiet life together. The marriage was suffering for some time, so Roger and Giovanna felt that it was time to get a divorce and move on with their lives. The couple had three children together: James Roger, Ellea, and Eliot Dante.

In the summer of 2004, two more Duran Duran DVDs were released under EMI, *Arena*, and *Sing Blue Silver*. They were both produced in Holland. Included with the *Arena* DVD are a movie poster and two pages of stickers with scenes from the film. *Sing Blue Silver* is in a velvet case. There are also a black and white postcard photographs of each original and member and a black and white photo book containing pictures of the band on tour.

Additional footage on the *Arena* DVD includes a TV ad, a trailer for the movie, the *Arena* video mix (which contained different scenes and songs from the film), and a 1985 interview with Simon. The interview consists of him talking about the band's need to be creative with their music. They wished to avoid literal translations of the words to the screen. Simon also made the statement that some of his early inspiration came from the punk rock movement. This is mainly because it proved the point that one does not have to be a brilliant musician to express his or her thoughts on the stage.

Also included is the film documentary *The Making of Arena*, which includes behind the scenes footage that pieced together the scenes of the film. They got the idea for *Arena* while performing the last show for their 1984 North American tour. The members of the band saw the cameras in front of them. They said they would like one of their performances to be filmed like a movie.

When Simon further discussed the film, he talked about the metaphor of pain and being forced to perform. For instance, he had to lip sync the words to "The Wild Boys" while being tied to the windmill. The premise of pain was one of the things on which the film was based.

The time between the reunion tour and the release of the new album seemed like an eternity to fans who'd anxiously awaited it. The reunion tour whetted the appetite of fans, who were waiting for the "main course to be served."

On October 12, 2004, the long wait was finally over. The Fab Five's first album in twenty-one years, *Astronaut*, finally hit stores in the United States. The album had not been given a name until July and was produced by Don Gilmore. This was the first album since *Liberty* that had a photograph of the entire band on the front cover.

The release of *Astronaut* allowed he band to triumph over any negative criticism they received. The album was also sold as a CD and DVD combo. The DVD was released by Epic Records and included footage of the band as the stage was being set up. They were getting ready to perform their first show at Wembley Arena, where they had not played since their sold-out performance of 1984.

Just as they had in *Sing Blue Silver*, they commented on fashion, their new videos, and their new look. Simon didn't even stop commentating while he was putting his pants on underneath his robe. The scene was tactfully edited as not to offend the viewing audience.

The last part of the DVD included feedback from some fans after the show at the Wembley Arena. Most of them expressed their excitement over the band's reunion. The many privileged fans were thrilled at having the opportunity to watch Duran Duran perform at the famous venue. Many fans were pleased with the success of *Astronaut*, and they were anxious to express their excitement, especially since they knew the band would continue the trend.

In late 2004, their music made another small appearance in the movie, *Shrek 2*. One of the bonus features on the DVD included a segment called *Far Far Away Idol* (whose judges included Shrek, Princess Fiona, and a medieval version of Simon Cowell), for which the characters from the movie sang popular songs. As one may easily guess, the Big Bad Wolf performed "Hungry Like the Wolf" for his segment; the Three Little Pigs sang backup vocals. (Of course, Simon had nothing nice to say about the performance for "Hungry Like the Wolf" or any of the other songs for that matter.)

Astronaut included elements of the band's eighties sounds along with modern techno created by new technology. The new album had what some thought others seemed to lack. *Astronaut* was different from *Medazzaland* and *Pop Trash* because it had more of a techno sound. Nick's keyboards are strong throughout the album. One can listen to *Astronaut*, knowing that the incorporation of technology plays a large part of the music. Simon's voice sounds more like an instrument

The Strongest Comeback!

when Andy's guitar starts playing the novelty song, "Bedroom Toys." Fans can have positive associations relating the instruments to their respective band members.

Some claim that *Astronaut* was so named because Duran Duran's character in *Barbarella* was an astronaut from planet earth. A few months before the album was released, the song "(Reach Up for the) Sunrise" became a big hit. The "Jason Nevins Remix" was featured on the popular television show *Queer Eye for the Straight Guy*. The show consisted of five homosexual men whose task was to improve the living conditions of their straight counterparts.

Interestingly enough, the five men who starred in the show were also given the nickname the "The Fab Five." While many fans had mixed reactions to this new claim, they kept it in their minds that Duran Duran was the real Fab Five who had earned their title as a result of their early fame.

The promotion "(Reach Up for the) Sunrise" had from the show made people aware of the first single to be included on their upcoming album. The video was also viewable on VH1 and the Internet a few months before *Astronaut* was released. Its visuals are captivating and spectacular.

While certain images in the video were made to appeal to the twenty-something crowd, other elements are reminiscent of ones from their early videos. The song reached No.1 on the Billboard Dance Chart.

The next big hit single was "What Happens Tomorrow," which some fans compare to "Ordinary World." The single was released in January 2005. The video for the single portrays a theme of mystery and uncertainty. A young couple gazes at the stars as they continue to contemplate their own fate.

Fans all over the world were anxious to see where the album would fall on the charts. In England and Australia, the album placed on No.2 and No.4 respectively. People living in the United States hoped the album would climb up a few spots after a few more weeks on the market. Even though the album never reached any higher than No.17, the overall success of the album was great. *Astronaut* was the second biggest selling album since *The Wedding Album*.

They were invited back on various television shows for brief interviews and performances of their new hit "(Reach Up for the) Sunrise." Their next single "Whatever Happens Tomorrow" was frequently played shortly after the release of the album. Many fans were already familiar with it because it had been played on tour. It also received airtime on the radio and through the Internet.

The success of *Astronaut* did something for the fans as well as the band. It brought back those who had not seen Duran Duran perform for over twenty years. Many younger fans found themselves discovering the band, a lot of them for the first time.

Throughout the span of his career, numerous comments have been made about Simon's escalating weight. The singer maintained that he tries to keep himself in good shape through better food selection and exercise. Unfortunately, his weight has always been a target for those wishing to make fun of him.

In 1993, *SNL* aired a sketch in which Chris Farley portrayed Simon, greatly exaggerating his size. Simon agrees that since he is in a profession where fans would be seeing him on tour and in videos, he knows how crucial it is to maintain his appearance. It is the general opinion that everyone in the band did a good job maintaining their appearance over the years. Many fans may agree that their looks are still a part of their deadly combination.

In a way, Nick figured that their new sound would capture the attention of the younger fans. He also knew that many attending the shows remained with them since their early days of fame. The combination of all these types of fans drawn together was enough to raise the noise level clear to the roof. The fact that all the band members maintained their looks is enough to prove that Duran Duran has physically withstood the test of time. Simon's voice still affects fans the same way.

Unfortunately, those who do not appreciate the value of *Astronaut* claim that the popular singles, "(Reach Up for the) Sunrise," and "What Happens Tomorrow" have yet to reach the calibre of older hits, such as "Hungry Like the Wolf," and "Rio." "(Reach Up for the) Sunrise" and "What Happens Tomorrow," although they were released before the album, they didn't have nearly enough time to get as much acclaim as their early counterparts. Since both new singles each received such little airplay, the band's official website listed radio stations that would play them.

Even though some may have thought the situation looked bleak, Nick has stated that the band started to relax a little more because they built up their name tremendously since their beginnings in 1978.

While they displayed fear of their new singles not becoming big hits, they were confident in their talent.

A second box set, *The Singles 1986-1995*, was released in North America by EMI on November 2, 2004. It contains their hits from 1986 to 1995. A few of the biggest songs include "Notorious," "Burning the Ground," and many variations of singles from the *The Wedding Album*. The box set has a total of fourteen discs, each containing anywhere from three to eight songs. Other featured songs include popular B-sides, such as "We Need You" and "Yo Bad Azzizi."

As a fan, it's refreshing to find that other bands admire the Fab Five. Some of these other bands and performing artists who attribute their success to Duran Duran include Live and the Barenaked Ladies. Gwen Stefani also stated that she has been an admirer of Duran Duran's music for years.

Two other bands who share their fond admiration are Franz Ferdinand and the Killers. The latter of the two borrow a lot of their material from eighties new wave music. They especially admire Duran Duran for their great contributions. The fact that so many other musicians like Duran Duran makes Simon, in turn, admire them.

Although many argue that musicians should not include political messages in their songs, Duran Duran wanted to make a statement based on a current event. Their song, "Point of No Return," talks about Bush's decision to bomb Baghdad. The band blatantly disagreed with his decision. Some who listened to the song also might have thought that it referred to the tragic events of September 11th.

Although 9/11 is not debated in the song, the band got their message across. Simon is always the type to keep up with current events. He, along with the other band members, always feel it's important to express their thoughts through music. Things like this have always been important to Duran Duran, and they feel they need to be in touch with the world around them.

Close to Thanksgiving of 2004, Andy suffered some health problems and was ordered to bed rest until after New Year's Day. For a while, fans were kept in the dark about what exactly was going on. Rumours began to circulate that Andy had never completely gotten over the disease he caught in Sri Lanka.

He was temporarily replaced by Londoner Dominic Brown. His first appearance on television seemed to be a small one because the cameramen focused on the original members of the band. They rarely showed shots of Dominic as he performed on stage. People watching television from home may have found themselves curious about the new guitarist after they noticed Andy's disappearance.

Dominic Brown started playing guitar at the age of fourteen. He made music his full-time vocation. Shortly after Dom finished college, he started a band with his father, Rob Brown (formerly of Getz Loose). Dominic took over singing vocals. Father and son often experimented with blues and R&B sound, and they were renowned for their unique stage personas.

As he became known for his singing, Dom toured England and France. In the latter of the two, he found success in playing festivals and receiving frequent airplay. Even though Dom is a performer, first and foremost, he makes the assertion that song writing is his greatest love.

He also performed shows at various clubs, such as This Whisky-A-Go-Go, The Roxy, and the Troubadour. Dominic has worked with famous artists such as Appleton, Beenie Man, Emma Bunton, Elton John, Amy Studt, Rod Stewart, Eddy Grant, Eagle Eye Cherry, and Archive.

No sooner than when Andy returned to the band, Roger had an accident. He broke the fifth metatarsal bone in his right foot and was ordered to rest for several weeks. On January 13, 2005, a show at the Hammersmith Palais, was taped so it could be broadcast on U.S. radio. Roger's foot was in great pain and swollen from the performance, so he was ordered to rest for an additional period.

Roger also released a public apology, stating he was sorry the shows had to be cancelled. He was especially sorry for the fans who travelled from around the world to see these shows. Shortly after, those who had paid for the concerts were refunded their money. The band was onstage performing a show in Atlanta, Georgia, when Roger tripped on the stage. They had to cancel their upcoming Japanese tour, but they returned in time for the *Astronaut* Tour, which kicked off in Puerto Rico on February 8, 2005. The band began their eight-week tour of the United States only weeks later.

Wes Wehmiller passed away in February 2005 in California. He was thirty-three years old. Wes was in Duran Duran from 1997 to 2001, after which he followed Joe Travers to perform with Warren Cuccurullo and Dale Bozzio. Wes portrayed his talent at a young age and attended the Berkley College of Music, where he formed his own band, I, Claudius. He had no hard feelings toward Duran Duran after he left because he knew he always wanted to establish his name and write his own songs. Wes made a great contribution to Duran Duran, and he is surely missed by all his fans.

Unfortunately, Andy had also suffered a great loss. His father Ron died of a heart attack in hospital on March 22, 2005. Andy returned to Newcastle when he heard the news of his father's illness. He was originally told that Ron was on the verge of death, and if he wanted to see him before he passed away, he would have to go back to England as soon as possible.

Once the other band members learned of the situation, they showed their genuine concern and asked if they should cancel the rest of the American tour dates. Andy was touched that his band mates and friends took him into consideration, but he told them that a cancellation would not be necessary. He wanted the band to carry on, even if it meant his absence for a few of the shows.

The other members of the band were also shaken by the news, but they stood by Andy during his time of need. They knew he would soon return to play the rest of the dates. Simon made announcements to the audiences during Andy's absence.

He told them what Andy said about sticking to the tour and it generated a positive response from the crowd. It showed that Andy still held within him the true spirit of the band, which, some may say, never left him in the first place. Andy has always felt a great sense of dedication to his family, so he left as soon as he could.

Dominic Brown took over for some of the *Astronaut* Tour dates, but Andy fully resumed his spot in the band fully after his father's funeral. The band's official fan community website, www.duranduranmusic.com, took donations in memory of Ron Taylor.

Due to the album's success and Duran Duran's upcoming tour, *Astronaut* was re-released as a CD/DVD combo. The second DVD contained different material from what was first included, and the main topic included information about the reunion. After an account of how the reunion occurred, each member of the band expressed their thoughts about the others. They emphasised how they were glad to be working with each other again.

The next segment included footage on the making of "(Reach Up for the) Sunrise." Each member shared their philosophy about making music. They found they agreed on many things, especially the fact that they were most committed as a band during the production of *Astronaut*. Although the title track was not released as a single, they are very fond of the song and think that it is one of the best tracks from the album.

During the promotion of *Astronaut*, the band was seen signing albums and chatting with the fans who had been lucky enough to meet them. Then, the camera scanned the lines of fans who eagerly expressed their enthusiasm, which is far from seeing their last days of fame.

Anticipation filled the air as they prepared to kick off their US tour. Fans waited in lines at ticket vendors and went online early in hopes of being the first ones to purchase great tickets. Through both fan club and regular sales, the band successfully sold out many shows. They closed the first part of the American tour on April 13 in New York City.

They performed in Europe in May and June. The band resumed their US tour on July 15, and it lasted through the fall of 2005. Before they started the second part of the tour in the United States, they performed their only show scheduled in England at Birmingham City Football Club's St Andrews ground on May 28, 2005.

A very surprising piece of news was revealed to Duranies on May 16, 2005. Simon made the announcement, at a press conference in Glasgow, that he would enter with the Drum in another race. The crew of the vessel reunited and took part in the Rolex Fastnet Yacht race on August 7, 2005. The race started in the Isle of Wight. It was reported that a total of 250 yachts were entered in this event.

The Drum reunion marked the twentieth anniversary of the near tragic incident. The long list of the crew members who survived the event and participated in the race include Skip Novak, John Fitzgerald, Phil Wade, John Irving, Paul Berrow, Mike Berrow, Terry Gould, Rick Tomlinson, Chris Baker, Max Bourgeois, Roger Nilson, Phil Holland, Neil Cheston, Bruno Peyron, Pascal Pellet Finet, Chas From Tas, Trevor Dowe, Phil Barret, John Le Bon, Simon Le Bon, Johnson Woodison, Malcolm McKeag, John Toon, Micke Olsen and Magnus Olson. The yacht was renamed for the man who loaned it to Simon, Sir Arnold Clark. The boat was then called the "Arnold Clark Drum." Arnold was enthusiastic about the plan, and he hoped to see Simon and the others at the finish line.

Simon took some time off from his tour schedule to focus on the race. Since the race began on August 7, 2005, that allowed only five days for Simon to re-join the rest of the band. They were scheduled to play a show in Japan. Simon stated that he looked forward to reuniting with the original crew and declared that he wanted to finish the race the second time around. Simon, however, withdrew early so he and his band mates could prepare for their Japanese tour.

A film company by the name of Jacaranda Films purchased the rights to the film which was made aboard the yacht for this year's race. Two camera crews used cutting edge technology, including cameras with night vision, to film the entire twenty-four hours of the race. Some other exciting parts of the film included interviews with the cast and footage from the race in 1985. This was shown in a one-hour documentary about the yacht and its crew as they finally completed the race which they started over twenty years earlier.

Those who were involved looked forward to the reunion, but some fans were hesitant to show their enthusiasm. Many questioned Simon's decision, and they wondered why he would embark again on something this dangerous.

Simon claimed his decision was based on gratitude. He and the other members of the crew felt that a small statement was not enough to express how thankful they are to the men who saved their lives. They also wanted the whole world to know about the devotion of the crew because they supported the RNLI charitable cause. The crew was also determined to finish the race. For twenty years, Simon waited to fulfil his dream, and he finally received his opportunity to do so.

At this time, there were rumours that Bob Geldof was planning another large event similar to 1985's Live Aid. Their intention was to raise millions of dollars to help alleviate famine in Africa. Up until May 26, 2005, he denied these rumours. Shortly after, Bob finally revealed some plans for his upcoming event while attending the Ivor Novello Awards, which honoured songwriters in London. He relayed his information to The Associated Press and emphasised that the event was going to be nothing like a Live Aid II because Live Aid was very unique.

Elizabeth Freund, the spokesperson for the concert in the United States, said that Bob would announce more details about the event on May 31. This was the day he announced that Duran Duran would be part of the large event.

The concerts were performed in five cities throughout the world,

Philadelphia, London, Berlin, Paris, and Rome. Instead of performing in Philadelphia like they did for *Live Aid*, Duran Duran played in Rome.

Others who participated in the event included Madonna, U2, Paul McCartney, Oasis, The Rolling Stones, Elton John, Eminem, R.E.M., Bon Jovi, Dave Matthews, Stevie Wonder, Lauren Hill, Brian Wilson, and Pink Floyd, who reunited for the show. The reunion of Pink Floyd was very highly anticipated, since it was their first time on stage together with Roger Waters since 1981.

Initially Bob Geldof was reluctant to reveal any more information because he wanted to get his facts straight. Sting was the first performer to confirm his participation in the event.

At first, the organiser didn't reveal the exact date the event was to take place. It was originally planned for July 3rd because the charity's annual Party in the Park event was cancelled at Hyde Park in London. The spokesperson for the England Prince's Trust cancelled their event for the day so Bob could hold what was going to be called Live 8, which took place on July 2, 2005.

The organisation and logistics in planning the event were enormous, but Bob wanted to prove his point while including the biggest names in music of the day. He also decided the concerts would be free admission because the whole idea of the event was to raise awareness in developing countries. When the press questioned Bob about his decision, he stated that the number of people who attended the show was more important than having to be concerned with an admission price.

He felt if people became more aware of the situation, then they would be more likely to try and help do something about it. Bob and the others were more concerned about getting their message out to the public so that people knew what the entire purpose of the concerts was.

It was later announced that a sixth country would host a concert. This concert took place on July 6, 2005 in Edinburgh, Scotland. The decision was made by the leaders of the G8 group of wealthy nations. They also decided that they would give their concert a different name, The Long Walk to Justice concert. 60,000 free tickets for the event were given away on a text lottery. Those who performed at the event included: Snow Patrol, Dido, and Annie Lennox and the Proclaimers. Other talent included various well-known Scottish groups.

The Strongest Comeback!

Duran Duran's set list for Live 8 included "(Reach Up for the) Sunrise," "Ordinary World," "Save a Prayer," and "The Wild Boys." July 13, 2005 marked the 20th anniversary of the original *Live Aid*.

The Drum reunion and Live 8 provide an interesting parallel between past and current events. First, Simon announced that he wanted to re-join the original crew of the Drum so he could finish the race that he started twenty years ago.

Then, Bob Geldof announced another charity concert. Many may find it coincidental that these events happened nearly twenty years apart. It's interesting that Duran Duran decided to regroup in 2000, twenty years after they formed their Fab Five line-up. By 1984, the band was on top of the world. Twenty years later, the release of *Astronaut* helped them re-establish their fan base. It seemed in these cases history nearly repeated itself.

Shortly after the *Astronaut* Tour ended, the band returned to the studio to start work on their next album. Having recently enjoyed the success of their *Astronaut* Tour, the band was determined to get to create another album which would generate just as much fan interest.

While the Internet has helped Duran Duran, (and its solo members) boost their careers since the mid-nineties, there is another aspect which has become very popular during the last few years, YouTube. The site was launched in February 2005, and users have posted countless videos, pertaining to almost anything imaginable. One can easily search Duran Duran and find a good number of videos, clips, and interviews which have only remotely anything to do with the band. YouTube is a great resource, as many people can come together to post and comment on various visual content.

On November 1, 2005, another Duran Duran DVD was released. *Duran Duran: Live from London* was recorded at Wembley Arena during the band's *Astronaut* Tour. The concert started off with white lights pulsing through the air. All five members of the band stood still on the stage to the sound of a heart beating. Some fans may even go so far as to say that this parallels the opening of the concerts for the *Strange Behaviour* Tour.

Not surprisingly they serenaded the audience with their previous hits, as the only two new songs they performed were "(Reach Up for the) Sunrise" and "What Happens Tomorrow." Needless to say, however, the fans did not seem disappointed by this. The fact that Duran Duran can still sell out their shows at large venues indicates that they still know how to reach their fans.

The concert is a CD/DVD set, which also includes a photo inlet, along with perforated and detachable 3-D glasses. The photos present a panoramic view of Wembley Arena, spanning across the large number of fans who attended the concert. Also, there are a few photos of the band onstage.

On May 15, 2006, a compilation album entitled *Only After Dark* was released. Its intent was to portray the band's early days as they performed in the Rum Runner. Even though Nick Rhodes and John Taylor were credited as artists, the album is really a compilation of electro tunes from the late seventies and early eighties (much to the chagrin of Duranies, who thought that this was a remix CD or compilation album). There are eighteen tracks in total. Some of the songs included on the album are "Underpass" by Jamie Foxx, "I Feel the Love," by Donna Summer, and "Always Crashing the Same Car," by David Bowie.

A small booklet was included with the CD, and it opens up to reveal a photograph of the artists included on the album; Nick and John are seen right in the centre. A few of the artists whose songs are on the album include; David Bowie, Donna Summer, Grace Jones, and the Psychedelic Furs.

A printed introduction by Nick Rhodes is on the inside sleeve of the jewel case. In the introduction, he talks about his early days as a DJ at the Rum Runner. Punk and glam rock had enjoyed increased popularity during this time, and Nick was well aware of this fact since he was a DJ at the club. All the songs on the album were personally selected by Nick, as they, along with many others, were played at the Rum Runner. Nick meant for this to be a tribute to the Rum Runner, as Duran Duran was starting to establish their musical career.

CHAPTER 13

Saying Goodbye for a Second Time

On October 25, 2006, Simon, Nick, John, and Roger announced that Andy was no longer going to be part of the band, again. During that weekend, their partnership officially dissolved. The band made the statement that they could no longer work together due to their difference of opinions.

Dominic continued with the rest of the American dates until the tour came to an end on November 11, 2006. Sadly, the new Fab Five line-up was very-short-lived. Even though Roger had originally stated that he would re-join only if Andy came back, Roger decided to stay in the band after Andy announced that he was leaving again.

The trouble started when Andy planned on boarding a plane headed to New York City in September 2006. He was going to join the rest of the band, who had recently started work on their next album, *Red Carpet Massacre*. It was during this time when he found out that the band's management had failed to secure his visa, which would allow him to enter and work in the United States. If all that wasn't enough, all the band members were fighting over the money and royalties they'd received from *Astronaut*.

The whole thing about the band's management failing to secure Andy's visa was enough to have Andy reconsider his place in the band. This prompted him to write an angry e-mail to the band's management: he also sent a copy to Simon. In the e-mail, Andy explained how very unhappy he was with the entire situation.

A few weeks later, the Duran Duran website announced that Andy had left the band once again. Dominic Brown took over playing guitar for the band and has remained with them since 2006.

Before Andy departed again, they started work on the follow-up to *Astronaut*. *Reportage* was to be the name of the "new album." According to Andy, the band had been offered to record on a $450 million yacht owned by Microsoft co-owner Paul Allen. The plans fell through, however, and they had to find another place to record. The band had settled on tennis player Andre Agassi's San Francisco mansion and began recording in September 2005. *Reportage* was recorded between September 2005 and April 2006.

Nick mentioned how they enjoyed working on the album, as it contains Andy's last work with the band. A complete song list for *Reportage* includes; "Criminals In the Capitol," "48 Hours Later," "Transcendental Mental," "Traumatized," "Angel Fire," "Under the Wire," "Judy, Where Are You?," "Naomi Tonight," "You Ain't Foolin' No One," "Cathedral," "Faster," "Finally," "Lions and Wolves," "Midnight City," "Under Snow."

At first, John was the one who was really excited about making a new album, having just wrapped up another tour. He was the one who was essentially in charge of the recording session. The band enjoyed the fact that they could produce the album themselves.

Nick described *Reportage* as being edgy, and he said that the sound went back to the band's earlier roots. From the description, it sounds like the songs on *Reportage* may be a mixture of *Duran Duran* and *Rio*. It also makes one wonder if it's at all like any of their newer albums, like *All You Need Is Now* or *Paper Gods*?

Nick, however, went on to further imply that the album is full of political references and anger, as there are songs which deal with political corruption and the state of the world. John backed Nick up on his opinion.

Simon brought up a few songs of which he is most proud: "48 Hours Later," "Transcendental Mental," and "Traumatized." However following Andy's departure production ceased and the album remains unreleased.

On May 7, 2007, Roger Taylor married his Peruvian fiancé, Gisella Bernales. Their Caribbean wedding took place at the Jalousie Plantation in St. Lucia. Simon Le Bon, Nick Rhodes, and John Taylor were all in attendance. The bridesmaids included Ellea Taylor, and Giuliana and Melissa, sisters of the bride. Gisella's father, Fernando Bernales, is a diplomat based out of Washington D.C. The couple met 2005 and started dating shortly after. Roger and Gisella's first child, Julian Roger, was born on July 9, 2011.

On July 7, 2007, the very first Live Earth charity event was held. Live Earth is an organisation formed by Kevin Wall, in partnership with

Al Gore. The whole idea behind the project is to use entertainment, which transcends time and culture, to get people to take action concerning the environment. The original event was dubbed: Live Earth: The Concerts for a Climate Crisis, and it was deemed as one of the most watched online events to date. Live Earth was a concert which was heard and seen all around the world.

Similar to Live Aid and Live 8, Live Earth held concerts at many different sites. In 2007, the concerts took place in the following eight locations; Giants Stadium, East Rutherford, New Jersey, USA; Copacabana Beach, Rio De Janeiro, Brazil; Wembley Stadium, London, UK; HSH Nordbank Arena, Hamburg, Germany; Oriental Pearl Tower, Shanghai, China; To-Ji Buddhist Temple, Kyoto, Japan; Coca-Cola Dome, Johannesburg, South Africa; and at the Aussie Stadium, Moore Park, Sydney Australia. Duran Duran held their performance at Wembley Stadium.

Other famous acts who performed at the venue included Genesis, The Beastie Boys, The Black Eyes Peas, The Foo Fighters, and Madonna. Live Earth has been held annually ever since and it continues to flourish, as many performers are proud to be part of the event.

****

Starting afresh after Andy's departure, the new recordings that were to make up the *Red Carpet Massacre* album were released in November 2007. The band had collaborated with famous personnel, such as Timbaland and Justin Timberlake, to work on their new songs. Although *Red Carpet Massacre* was highly anticipated, it was a far cry from some of Duran Duran's earlier works. The album was reported to have sold 71,000 copies, which was overall disappointing.

Members of the band think that part of the reason why *Red Carpet Massacre* had not been successful was due to a change in musical direction. They had succumbed to the hip-hop style, popular today. Rather than the music being reminiscent of *Rio* or *Seven and the Ragged Tiger*, it was more closely related to hip-hop and rock. Again, Duran Duran was trying to keep current with the times by experimenting with more popular genres of music.

As was the case with *Astronaut*, fans had the option of purchasing *Red Carpet Massacre* as a CD or a CD/DVD combo. The CD/DVD combo includes the album, the DVD/documentary, a photo spread for the album artwork, an "all access pass" *Red Carpet Massacre* Tour sticker, and an additional photo spread, crediting all those who worked on the album. A lot of information is included about the album and the artwork. There are also clips from the filming of the video for "Falling Down."

The album was partially produced in Manhattan Studio Centers in New York City. Simon sang the song "Nite Runner" as a duet with Justin Timberlake. The band began recording a mere few days after Timberlake's album *FutureSex/LoveSounds* made its debut on the charts at No.1. In an interview, John Taylor also talked highly of Justin Timberlake, calling him one of the most talented musicians on the scene today.

Nick made groove-based tracks, which Timbaland helped form into songs. The band showed their fond admiration for Timbaland, especially John, who said he was the only producer that they really liked. Roger later added Timbaland was the first outsider who had been invited to work with the band in a long time. Another producer, Nate Hills, aka Danja, also helped write and co-produce many tracks for the album.

Dominic Brown played guitar on all tracks. Simon said that the album was experimental, and it was the fastest one that the band had made up until that date. It was produced between September 2006 and May 2007.

The idea for the artwork came to Nick when he was visiting one of his friends in the South of France. He saw these four beautiful Russian girls, all of whom he thought would look good on the album cover. With each of their consent, he went out and bought some actual red carpet, which was laid down right before the photo session. Nick had the girls strike different poses, some of which can be seen on the photo insert for the CD/DVD combo. The girls' names are Anna Stupak, Natalia Belova, Irena Artemova, and Masha Stupak. Anna is the girl who is featured on the album cover, although her identity is slightly masked.

After Nick had finished taking the photographs, he played around with different images before sending the photos to Patty Palazzo. Patty added even more to the images, as she made red lines which were meant to look like police tape at a crime scene. The final product was supposed to resemble a news story. John made the claim that the band wanted the album not to be taken too seriously, which is why they incorporated some sex and dark humour.

The video for "Falling Down" was filmed at the Linda Vista Community Hospital in Los Angeles, California, which is a popular filming location. The video took a long time to make, as most everyone involved worked on it for eighteen hours. The characters are defined, as all the band members are doctors, and Simon plays the role of the head doctor.

The video features models who played nurses and patients, all of whom are delusional about their overall presence and appearance. One of the main characters of the video was said to represent popular female celebrities, such as Britney Spears or Lindsey Lohan. The DVD also includes commentary on the many celebrities who are constantly sent to rehab for their massive addictions.

John also added that his experiences in rehab were important, which may have served as further inspiration for the video. "Falling Down" was directed by Anthony Mandler, who has been a long-time fan of the band. Some of his outtakes were also included on the DVD. Gavin Elder filmed and directed "The Making of 'Falling Down'" segment.

Another feature included a photo session. The band had their pictures taken to the songs "Zoom In" and "Skin Divers" (for the NYC launch party). The photographs were taken for *Details* and *Nylon* Magazine.

Later commentary featured general discussion from the band about the music on *Red Carpet Massacre*. John said he had an affinity for the song "The Valley," which contains cerebral and in-depth lyrics. It is also said to be the theme song for the album. He also said that one has to really "dig in" to find the meaning behind the lyrics. Nick added that *Red Carpet Massacre* featured a different kind of music, which some fans may not have been accustomed to, but Duran Duran is always one band to experiment with different sounds.

The band played exclusively on Broadway at the Ethel Barrymore Theatre between November 1 and November 13, 2007. The shows consisted of three sets, the first of which was dedicated to the entire album *Red Carpet Massacre*.

The second focused on songs which were played on keyboard and synthesizer, making them sound like they were both retro and futuristic. During the third act, they played the hits for which they were most famously known. The shows were very well-received, and they were 90% sold-out shortly after word got out via press release.

While the shows turned out to be successful, the band's concert promoter, Ron Delsner, made the assumption that Duran Duran would break even. One of the reasons why the ticket prices ranged from $75-$150 is because of the large expense of playing on Broadway. Wendy Laister, of Magus Entertainment, said that Duran Duran would have had a hard time selling tickets for such "low" prices if they did not have a sponsor. Citi, the financial services company, provided sponsorship funds for the concerts.

The company initiated a Citi Pass Program, which enabled members to purchase pre-sale tickets and the opportunity to meet the band members. They also provided free advertising for their new album and money up-front for the Broadway concerts. Both the band and their management were very grateful for having received assistance from Citi.

In 2008, Andy Taylor wrote a biography about his life, *Wild Boy: My Life in Duran Duran*. In it, he mentions many things, including why he left the band for a second time. Andy also touches on different aspects of his personal life, and how he formed his decision to both re-join and leave the band once again. And, although Andy is no longer a member of Duran Duran, fans will always remember him as one of the band's successful, founding members.

Later during the same year, a new DVD was released, entitled: *Duran Duran: Classic Albums: Rio*. Rather than being a straight video compilation, *Rio* is a documentary describing the story behind most every aspect of the album. Not only is there commentary by the band, but it includes input from others who have worked with them, such as Bob Geldof, Dave Ambrose of EMI Records, and Paul Berrows. The documentary discussed everything from the album cover design of *Rio*, to making it big in America.

On July 7, 2009, Duran Duran, performed live at the Fillmore in San Francisco, California. And, even though this performance was between albums and tours, the band made fans anticipate the show all the more. As was also the case with many of their other performances, tickets sold out in a matter of minutes.

The concert lasted for two hours, and they filled most of the time slot by playing their hits, along with a few B-sides and newer tracks. Of course, the band was eager to have a summer tour and perform onstage, as they were between albums, but they probably did not expect the great reception they received from excited fans, some of whom may have been all too eager to revisit the eighties.

One of the songs the band performed was "Do You Believe in Shame?," and it was dedicated to Michael Jackson, who had recently passed away. Simon Le Bon was very pleased to perform at this venue, and he even told the audience how glad he was to be there.

Later that year, another DVD was released, called *Duran Duran Live at Hammersmith '82*. The concert was released as a CD/DVD combo. *Duran Duran Live at Hammersmith '82* was highly anticipated by fans, as it was previously unreleased. Certain fans also seemed to like the concert because it took them back to a time when Durandamonium was taking England by storm. One of the bonus tracks is a live cover of Cockney Rebels' 1975 hit "Make Me Smile (Come Up and See Me)." This compilation is truly a collector's item for many fans.

2009 was another sad year for John Taylor, as his father passed away on December 10. Jack's death was not quite as sudden as Jean's, but the trouble started when John received a phone call from his cousin Eddie one day, saying that his father had gone missing. He left the house around lunchtime and still had not returned several hours later. Since Jack liked to take a drive every day, Eddie had not thought much about it until mid-afternoon.

The police were notified, and Eddie filed a missing person's report. Luckily, Jack's car was picked up by a security camera at Royal Leamington Spa at about 4:00 in the afternoon.

Shortly after, John's dad began to talk in great detail about his experiences in WWII, which he had never relayed much to his son before. John was surprised to hear about all the hardships that soldiers had undergone during those times. Things had gotten even worse, and Jack began to lose his hearing. He even went on a hunger strike when his dear sister, Elsie, passed away.

It wasn't much longer before Jack's memory began to fade, and he passed on shortly after that. Sadly, John was not in town when his father died. He was in New York with Mark Ronson; the two of them were in the middle of a recording session. He and Gela were woken by the phone and heard the horrible news. Simon sang an emotionally driven version of "Save a Prayer" at the funeral, and it was reported that everyone wept as a result of his performance.

In 2010, music writer Ron Sheffield published a book called

Talking to Girls About Duran Duran. Although the title may have seemed very promising to some Duranies, there is not as much mention of the band as one may think. The book mostly has to do with eighties music, and other eighties cultural references, in general.

Ron both critiques and praises the band for helping him understand the complexities of teenage girls in the eighties. *Talking to Girls About Duran Duran* is essentially a prequel to his 2007 memoir, *Love Is a Mix Tape*. Still, Sheffield's book is enough to capture the interest of most Duranies.

In the introduction, Rob makes the claim that he has always been a fan of Duran Duran. Needless to say, that is why he decided to write a book and dedicate a portion of it to the band. One thing that I found particularly interesting is when he talks about one of his female friends, Lisa, who is actually Julie Anne Friedman's cousin.

Lisa also attended Nick and Julie Anne's wedding in August 1984. So an intrigued Mark and another mutual friend, Heather, grilled Lisa for details; they were not disappointed at what she told them.

Of course, it has been disputed many times, over the years, whether or not Duran Duran is considered a "girlie band," and Mark will be one of the first ones to admit that women have always been the driving force behind their music. Females are the ones who respond to their sound, and they are also the ones who continue to experiment with music. Also, allegedly, many guys came to the concerts because they heard that they were popular hangouts for girls.

Another person who stated that Duran Duran was seen primarily as a girly band in the eighties is music journalist, Lyndsey Parker. Lyndsey is famous for her interviews and articles. Some other celebrities she has interviewed include people like Adam Lambert.

In her 2012 book, *Careless Memories of My Strange Behavior: My Notorious Life as a Duran Duran Fan*, Lyndsey made the assertion that many guys would not be caught dead listening to Duran Duran's music. And, if they did, other guys would call them "queer" for liking such girlie band. Now, it seems that it is much "safer" for straight guys to admit that they are fans, as attitudes toward the band have changed.

More men can now proudly proclaim that they are male Duranies because they like the music, and a lot of them attend concerts willingly instead of being dragged to them by their women. A good portion of Lyndsey's book is spent talking about the fact that Duran Duran didn't receive as much credit as they deserved, at least not until they began to fall out of popularity. That's when the music critics seemed to start liking their music. And, lots of guys in "masculine" bands, such as Limp Bizkit, No Doubt, and even The Bloodhound Gang even cite them as an inspirational source. That just goes to show how times can truly change.

Going back to the first book, Rob Sheffield made some more valid points. Mark and many other people who grew up during the eighties, however, often make the assertion that they are surprised that Duran Duran's career lasted longer than 1989. A few pages later, Mark talks very briefly about each band member, touching on notable things for which they are most famous. Here, he also pokes a little fun at the band just to make his readers laugh.

Duran Duran also made a lot of guys very cynical. Since they were one of the first bands who became known for their music videos, a lot of men didn't take them seriously. Part of this was also due to the band's good looks.

And these comments didn't come only from your average, everyday men. Musicians such as The Clash and The Sex Pistols spoke their minds about Duran Duran. John Lydon, of the Sex Pistols, even went so far as to say that he pitied female fans who were duped into buying their records. Even The Dire Straits' song "Money for Nothing" was a jab against the band, as they refer to them as, "the little faggots" playing to the masses on MTV. Of course, homophobia was much more rampant in the early eighties than it is now.

Mark then went back in time to talk about the 2003 *MTV Video Music Awards*. During that summer, he wrote a speech about Duran Duran and its achievements. He then talked about how Avril Lavigne and Kelly Osbourne presented the band with their award; all the while Mark is going to great lengths to emphasise how surprised each member was to receive such an honour.

Even the mere mention of Duran Duran's song titles sent the audience into near hysterics. Despite the slight ribbing by the author however, he makes the assertion that he is still a fan of Duran Duran, and he goes on to say what a big influence they have had on his life.

In September 2010, the Rock and Roll Hall of Fame announced their 2011 nominees. Unfortunately, Duran Duran was not among them. Even though the band has been around since 1978, (meeting the main criteria of their first studio album being twenty-five years or older) they were still overlooked for this great honour. One of the main arguments of those who want to see them inducted is the fact that they were one of the most significant bands to come out of the early 1980s. They were pioneers in the area of music video, as they have made many other important contributions to music, and they still do today.

While overlooking Duran Duran was a great oversight, other talented artists were snubbed as well. Currently, there is petition circulating around the Internet. Its aim is to get people to sign so that Duran Duran can finally get inducted.

In late 2010, Duran Duran made its way into another part of pop culture, well, at least part of them did. When the popular TV show, *Family Guy*, made its spoof of the third *Family Guy Star Wars* movie adaptation, *It's a Trap!*, there was a small reference to the Power Station.

The characters who were supposed to portray Lando Calrissian (Mort Goldman) and Nien Nunb (Rallo Tubbs, a Character from *The Cleveland Show*) were about to destroy the Death Star. In order to do so, they had to, "take out The Power Station." The camera then pans to the band playing their hit song, "Some Like It Hot," seconds before they are destroyed by a laser beam. The triumphant duo then escape the Death Star, completely unscathed, before it blows up.

Another animated D2 reference came earlier that year when a family movie, *Alpha and Omega* hit theatres. The story is about two wolves, on opposite ends of the chain, who are tranquilized and relocated to repopulate. The trailer for the movie includes portions of the song "Hungry Like the Wolf."

Despite the fact that Duran Duran underwent yet another transitional period after Andy left the band again, thus leaving them to deal with the overall disappointment of *Red Carpet Massacre*, they were determined to forge ahead. The band had some ideas for their next album, and they knew that they wanted to produce something different than what they had for their last few works. Duran Duran's next work was going to be something phenomenal. And, once again, they were going to take the world by storm.

CHAPTER 14

Going Back to Their Roots

Although *Red Carpet Massacre* proved to be a commercial disappointment, they were not ready to give up. Since the success of *Astronaut* proved that the band has staying power and was able to gain back the interest of their old fans, all did not seem lost. All they seemed to need was a simple "course correction" and move in the opposite direction from which they were going.

That's where the band's new producer, Mark Ronson, came in. Other musicians with whom the producer has worked with include Amy Winehouse and Adele. Mark Ronson has been a long-time Duran Duran fan. Ever since he was a child, he has been fascinated with their work, mostly because his mother was friends with the band. Years later, Mark's dream came true when he produced *All You Need Is Now*. Although he is extremely proud of this accomplishment, Mark remains modest and claims that he only gave the fans what they wanted to hear.

According to Roger Taylor, meeting Mark Ronson was purely by accident, after the band performed a show in Paris. What they liked most about Mark was the fact that he has been a fan since the eighties. The famous producer went on to explain that the first band he joined during his school days included the song "The Wild Boys" in their set. The band was impressed that Mark knew all the songs off their albums, as well as the B-sides. In essence, he was very familiar with Duran Duran's sound, the same sound which seemed to be missing since the 1980s.

In an interview, Roger mentioned that since they had regained their popularity, they wanted to maintain their fan base. They wanted to have the same sound as that of other artists and musicians being played on the radio. Ronson, however, was quick to encourage the band to return back to their original sound.

He essentially worked with each member and told them what he liked best about their music. For example, he got Simon to sing the same as he did on the early albums. Multi-tracking was used on his vocals to capture the old Duran Duran sound. The other members of the band were also encouraged to play their instruments like it was 1984 again.

The greatest thing about this particular album is the fact that through Mark's input they went back to their roots and recreated their original sound. This was quite a contrast to the poorly received *Red Carpet Massacre*.

Even the highly anticipated *Astronaut* did not have the same sound which made the band famous. John Taylor made the assertion that Duran Duran's music is mainly synth-pop with some guitar. Simon also had something to say about the new album; he claimed that the band received a message from their fans. They want to keep the flame alive and burning for many more years to come.

Just as was the case with many of their other albums, they enlisted the help of other musicians, backing vocalists, etc. One example is the song "Safe (in the Heat of the Moment)," for which Ana Matronic, of Scissor Sisters, provides backing vocals. Another is the song "The Man Who Stole a Leopard," for which Nina Hossain of *ITN*, dictated a "news story" at the end.

Ronson said that he wanted to produce a Duran Duran album which the fans wanted to hear; that is the very reason why the members of the band, particularly Simon and Nick, thought he was their first natural choice for the new album's producer.

Although Ronson was the person often credited for planting the seed, Duran Duran was directly responsible for changing their music. Nick was interested in playing something new. The band wanted to have a jam, which, according to Ronson, they had not done since the days of *Rio* or *Seven and the Ragged Tiger*. Roger and John went back to the basics with the band and worked very hard to produce their "classic" sound.

A few examples which immediately come to mind are the songs "Girl Panic!," which sounds a little like "Girls on Film," and "Before the Rain," which slightly resembles "The Chauffeur." Also, both "A Diamond in the Mind" and "Return to Now" remind me of the John Barry movie score version of "A View to a Kill", all the more evidence that *All You Need Is Now* is the direct sequel to *Rio*.

In an interview, Simon also said that since Ronson was coming from a fan's perspective, his input was all the more valuable to the band. As a child, Ronson found himself slightly disappointed with *Seven and the Ragged Tiger* because it did not seem to live up to the expectations of the fans. Many seemed disappointed that the third studio album didn't sound like *Rio*. That was the main reason why Ronson pushed to the band to further experiment with their old sound.

He is quoted as saying that Duran Duran is as good as any young band making music today. He made the assertion based not only on the fact that the band returned to their old sound but also because of their staying power. Duran Duran is truly a remarkable band, not only because of all that they have accomplished but because of their large and loyal fan base.

Going back to the older days, Simon stated his opinion about their earlier work as compared to the new album. He says one of the reasons why the new album was so well-received is because of the fact that some consider it a follow-up to *Rio*. Since *Seven and the Ragged Tiger* was not quite the same as their acclaimed second album, *All You Need Is Now* was there to pick up the slack.

All You Need Is Now was released on iTunes in December 2010. The album debuted at No.2 on the iTunes download chart, which was even better than what *Astronaut* fared during the first week after its release. (The CD and LP versions were released in the United States in late February, which included extra tracks). In addition to the regular studio album, the band also released a CD/DVD version. The combination album contains an extra track, "Networker Nation."

"All You Need Is Now" is a great title track, as well as being the opening track of the album. Now that fans had another taste of "nostalgia" from hearing Duran Duran's classic sound, they wanted a musical video to accompany it. What both the video and the song seem to be saying is just that. "All you need is now" is a simple statement which indicates that the very moment which you are currently living is the most important moment in your life.

The video starts off with the band performing the song in black and white. The footage appears to be a little grainy. As the video progresses, young kids are shown walking down the street in full colour. They get together, go to clubs, etc., further indicating that they are caught up in the moment. The cameras captured a few more shots of the band, this time in colour, as they are moving about their lives. They are also caught up in the moment while enjoying everything which is going on all around them.

On March 23, 2011, Duran Duran performed live in Los Angeles, California. Kelis was featured on backup vocals. The video was directed by David Lynch as part of a musical series called *Unstaged*, which was an original series by American Express, who partnered with VEVO and YouTube. The Los Angeles show took place at the Mayan Theatre in Los Angeles, California. It coincided with the album's release, one day later, in stores. Duran Duran was the first band for which the series filmed a concert in Los Angeles. The band was able to sell out the performance in less than five minutes!

The video was streamed live from 10:00 a.m.-7:00 p.m., Eastern time. YouTube provided worldwide access to the live performance. This served as the first concert to kick off their *All You Need Is Now* tour. This was the first time that Duran Duran was on stage together since 2009. The video was available on YouTube but has since been removed

Filmmaker, David Lynch, was very excited about the project. One of his most notable credits was the 1977 movie *Eraserhead*, which John and Nick were really impressed with. Just like bands such as Pink Floyd started out doing in the sixties, David wanted to create images for the band. He wanted lots of shapes to fly around the camera as the band performed their set. Simon, as well as others, were all very enthusiastic about the project, and they expressed their excitement about David being in charge of it. Simon made the assertion that he and the rest of the band members were glad to help David achieve his vision.

Unstaged saw its beginnings in 2010, and the performance marked their fourth live stage show. Musical acts which the series featured before Duran Duran included Arcade Fire, John Legend & The Roots and Sugarland. All these artists combined got *Unstaged* nominated for eight Grammy nominations and four Grammy wins at the 53rd Grammy awards. And even though Duran Duran didn't reach No.1 on the Billboard charts like two of the other acts, it certainly helped fans regain their interest in the band, as it was a spectacular and well-received performance.

September 2011 saw the beginnings of the *All You Need Is Now* tour with four shows at small UK venues; September 1, The Old Fire Station, Bournemouth; September 8, The Junction, Cambridge; September 9, Trinity, Bristol; and September 10, The O2 Academy,

Oxford.

The band used these four simple performances to whet the appetites of fans who anticipated the actual tour. Many fans did not seem to care that the shows lacked the same kind of production value as compared to one of their regular concerts; they were just glad they had the chance to see their favourite band on stage.

They had many ups and downs during 2011. While the band successfully completed their six-week American tour, problems arose shortly after that. In May, Simon had problems with his vocal cords. The band had to cancel a lot of dates and, because of that, they lost a few months. At first, Simon wanted to give up singing altogether, which was certainly cause for concern.

John thought that this was going to be the end of the band. After a few months of resting, however, he was ready to get the show back on the road. Simon said that he was grateful to have received the treatment which enabled him to recover. He, along with many of the fans, were excited to get the ball rolling again.

They returned to the UK to perform twelve arena concerts in November 2011. The leg of this tour started on November 30 at the Brighton Centre. And, even though *All You Need Is Now* was released on iTunes nearly a year before the Brighton concert, Duran Duran was able to once again retain the interest of their fans.

November 18, 2011 was a day of honour for Nick, as he received a special acknowledgement. The University of Bedfordshire awarded him with an honorary degree for his contribution to the music world. Nick was acknowledged as a songwriter, performer, and producer, and he certainly deserved an honorary degree for all is hard work.

Since Duran Duran has always been known for their cutting-edge videos, they decided to do something different for their second single off the new album, "Girl Panic!" The video was published on YouTube on November 8, 2011. It's had over 5 million views as of February 1, 2012. The video was directed by Jonas Åkerlund and was filmed at the Savoy Hotel in London.

Not only does this version of "Girl Panic!" have some interesting visuals, but actual girls are the stars of the show. While Simon, Nick, John, and Roger are the ones doing the interviews, supermodels are the ones playing instruments and taking credit for writing the songs. There are many beautiful women featured in the video, and the four main models playing the parts of the band members are Naomi Campbell as Simon Le Bon, Eva Herzigová as Nick Rhodes, Cindy Crawford as John Taylor and Helena Christensen as Roger Taylor.

Ironically, "Simon" (Naomi) is the one who confessed that Duran Duran was the first band to have models star in their videos. Right after she makes that statement, short flashes of Duran Duran's most famous videos flash across the screen, including clips of "Girls on Film," "Notorious," and "Ordinary World."

"John" (Cindy) also says that Duran Duran has gone through many guitar players because she never knows who's going to show up next. Obviously, this is a reference to Andy Taylor having left the band twice, Warren Cuccurullo joining then leaving, and Dominic Brown taking over. The interviewer also tells "Nick" (Eva) that people have labelled him the world's first metrosexual, to which she quickly replies that she didn't know that.

Yasmin also makes three brief appearances. The first one during which she appears in front of the camera and says that she is not a member of Duran Duran. Some could state that she is either adding to the irony due to the fact that she is Simon's wife, or she is playing the part of Andy Taylor.

The second one is when she makes the claim that everything just seemed to fall into place.

For Yasmin's third appearance, she shows up in the photo shoot for a faux cover of *Harper's Bazaar* Magazine. The video then goes back and for the between the models and the actual band playing their instruments.

Not only does "Girl Panic!" have some interesting visual elements, it also portrays stereotypes of rock 'n' roll stars. Some might say that it is a well-known fact that rock stars and (super)models tend to go hand-in-hand.

Also, the women portraying Duran Duran in the video indulge themselves in hedonistic pleasures, such as drinking/drugs, sex, and partying. In some of the shots where the boys are playing employees of the hotel, they are subjected to the actions of the "surrogate band," as Nick wheels Helena in on a cart, and Roger is "molested" in an elevator by two girls, who are party guests!

So, in essence, "Girl Panic!" is a video within a video. And rather than portraying a straight narrative, like most other Duran Duran videos, this one is laid out more like a documentary. The fact that "Girl Panic!" is different from the ones that made the band famous in the eighties makes it all the more interesting and special.

Duran Duran partnered with an organisation called GAFTTA (Gray Area Foundation for the Arts) to create a visual project called *Here Right Now*. The premise of the entire project is to get fans to upload their feelings about their now, which are responses from single word prompts. *Right Here Now* was launched at Munich's DLD (Digital Life Design) conference. This is specifically for members of the fan community. Once it gathers all the fans' contributions, the project's goal is to portray different perceptions of words, ideas, and events as seen by many different people around the world.

Another live DVD was released in early July 2012. The show was filmed at the MEN Arena in Manchester on December 16, 2011. The name of the compilation is *A Diamond in the Mind – Duran Duran – A Performance – 2011*. The video was directed by Gavin Elder. The DVD includes the live concert, including "Come Undone" and "Is There Something I Should Know?" listed as bonus tracks. An extra physical feature of the Blu-Ray DVD includes a booklet of photos, song listings, and credits.

The interview, which can be accessed through the bonus features section, was also done by Gavin Elder. It gives the viewer some more insight into both the featured concert and the entire tour. Each member of the band got to have some input, as they all talked about 2011 in general. Nick was very proud to be part of such an innovative and interactive tour, and he was also happy that *All You Need Is Now* generated more interest in the band.

Simon said that they had a great year, despite the fact that he lost his voice. John made the assertion that Simon had overcome his challenge, and he came back even stronger. The band then talked about filmmaker David Lynch and how he had done such a good job with filming *American Express Unstaged*.

Roger made the statement that he was like another member of the band. Other parts of the interview included the band talking about Simon and how he struggled with his temporary voice loss and recovery, the *All You Need Is Now* tour, and the general feeling that the band got with another great success.

The highlights from the concert were great. The opening credits start off with "Return to Now" as the band gets ready to perform. There are different shots of the venue, and one of the cameras gets close up to four faces, which hung near the screens and had the band's images digitally projected onto them. A few interesting highlights from the concert included an updated version of the anime video shown during "Careless Memories" and the band sampling Frankie Goes to Hollywood's "Relax." Others who performed with the band onstage included Anna Ross singing backup, Simon Willescroft on saxophone, and Dawne Adams on percussion. The end credits run as "A Diamond in the Mind" is played.

They wrapped up their Australian tour in March 2012; that particular leg of the tour was a great success. The band had not performed there in five years. When they launched into the concert at the Rod Laver Arena in Melbourne, even after they started performing their new songs, such as "Before the Rain," the excitement level of the fans seemed to soar through the roof. Since the great success of *All You Need Is Now* broke out across the world, fans were eager to hear the new music, with their old sound.

Along with Snow Patrol, Stereophonics and Paolo Nutin they headlined the 2012 Olympics BT London Live Opening Ceremony Celebration Concert at Hyde Park on July 27. The Mayor of London, The Royal Parks and The London Borough of Tower Hamlets formed a partnership in order to plan a complete program of events. BT London Live broadcasted live sports events throughout the Olympic Games. The main objective of this event was to allow the public free access to watch Olympic sporting events while being entertained by the music headliners.

The event coincided precisely with the opening of the London Olympics Games of 2012. The musicians had to follow a strict time constraint. The BBC aired the competing athletes, the playing of the Olympic Anthem, entry and raising of the Olympic flag, and the lighting of the Cauldron and the Olympic flame.

For all those who missed the live performance, there are plenty of videos on YouTube of the band performing and talking about their performance.

September 2012 also saw the UK publication of John Taylor's autobiography, *In the Pleasure Groove: Love, Death, and Duran Duran*. Just as one may expect, the book is rich with personal and Duran history. I had a difficult time putting it down, which was probably the case with many other fans. In America it was published the following month. One can listen to John read several excerpts from the book on YouTube.

Going Back to Their Roots

Lyndsey Parker who has not only written a fan account of her days as a young Duranie entitled *Careless Memories of Strange Behavior: My Notorious Life as a Duran Duran Fan*, but she also wrote an article about American Idol contestant, Allison Iraheta.

Allison has formed a band called Halo Circus, whose members also include David Immerman and Matthew Hager. The latter of the two has worked with the likes of Scott Weiland, The Backstreet Boys, and Duran Duran. Another credit to the band includes the fact that one of Halo Circus' songs, "Something Special" was co-written by John Taylor. This is just another thing that keeps Duran Duran in the public eye.

On February 15, 2013, John was honoured with a very special award — The Experience, Strength, and Hope Award for the honest and touching recollections presented in his memoir, *In the Pleasure Groove*. He was sponsored by the Writers in Treatment, supported by New Directions in Women. The event was held at the Skirball Cultural Center in Los Angeles.

John was handed the award by long-time friend, actor Robert Downey Jr. Other such famous personnel who were there to support John included Ed Begley Jr., Bobcat Goldthwait, Ione Skye, and Divinia, who performed songs such as "Red Carpet Massacre," "Hungry Like the Wolf," and "Save a Prayer." Gela was also there, as were many other friends and fellow celebrities, such as Michael Des Barres, Steve Jones, Buzz Aldrin, and Kurtwood Smith.

Writers in Treatment is an organisation dedicated to helping recovering alcoholics and drug addicts discouraging negative behaviour and encouraging clean living. All the proceeds from the event went to Writers in Treatment Jewelle Sturm Memorial Scholarship Fund. John has certainly come a long way since his days in rehab. He entered rehab for thirty days and was released on December 15, 1994. John was very touched and honoured to receive such an award.

Elsewhere people have dug even deeper into the Duran Duran vaults and found yet another unreleased project done by part of the band. In 1996, Nick and Warren Cuccurullo collaborated on a project called *Bored with Prozac and The Internet?* The "album" was produced by TV Mania, Mark Tinley, and Anthony J. Resta and mixed by Bob St. John. The work contains eleven tracks, which consist of television samples and looped tracks.

One could even go so far to say that *Bored with Prozac and The*

Internet? is a concept album, along the lines of *Tommy*, *The Lamb Lies Down on Broadway*, or *The Wall*, although the sound is completely different. The overall story, however, is a little more reminiscent of The Who's *Lifehouse* because of the complete indoor resident(s) concept.

The basic story is that of a modern family giving up their privacy and freedom to a team of research scientists in exchange for a high-tech life and pop culture fame. Nick also said that they had a Broadway Musical in mind while making the album because it delved deep into the loves of the family. Each one had their own fascination. The father Ray was into religion. The mother, Cathy, addicted to prescription drugs. The daughter, Sassy, strives to achieve fame. The son, Snoop, is obsessed with computers, computer games, and hacking.

The scientists had the motive of studying the decline of modern society. And while this might have been a fairly new concept in the 1990s, some could say that it's a commentary about how people live their lives today.

The track listing for *Bored with Prozac and The Internet?* is; "What About God?," "Euphoria," "Beautiful Clothes," "You're Dreaming, Pal," "Paramount," "What's in the Future?" "I Wanna Make Films," "Yoghurt and Fake Tan," "Grab the Sun," "Using a Hidden Camera – Eyes in the Sky," "People Know Your Name."

When interviewed shortly before its release, Nick divulged some information about the album. While the three of them were working on *Medazzaland*, Simon began struggling with the concept of the new album. He got frustrated, and he suggested that they put the new album on hold. Nick and Warren agreed, but they did not want to stop working on *their* new project.

While Simon rested, the two of them started work on what was called *Planet Fashion*. Once everything was pieced together, Nick and Warren were impressed with the unique sound which came from the final work.

The executives at EMI/Capitol had different feelings about the album, however, because they said that they weren't really into that kind of sound. They'd hoped that Nick and Warren were delivering the new Duran Duran album.

In an interview, Nick stated that after the band finished work on the album, they put it on the backburner with the intention of releasing it between albums. Of course, once the band started to regain their old popularity, they had completely forgotten about it. It wasn't until around 2011 when Nick found the album when looking through the items in storage. What better time than after the massive success of *All You Need Is Now*?

The album was released for download on March 12, 2013. It was also released the previous day as a vinyl and limited-edition box set of 100 copies. A promotional video "Euphoria" was made and posted on YouTube. It was directed by Dutch Rall and Jean Renard. Miss Mosh is the blonde female starring in the video. There is also footage of Nick and Warren on YouTube.

On February 25, 2013, TV Mania posted a promo link for *Bored with Prozac and the Internet?* on YouTube. The picture consists of different images of TVs containing the words "TV Mania" on the screen. The video is just under five minutes long with samples of the songs following one another.

Some of the added features of the vinyl albums include Polaroid pictures taken and autographed by Nick, screen printed artwork, including a booklet of exclusive imagery, and some text written by Warren Cuccurullo. The front cover was illustrated by Vania Zouravliov.

The regular vinyl album includes three records. The regular records, Sides A through D, are pressed in white vinyl. There are also printed messages on the run out grooves. Sides A-D all contain separate, little messages, which seem to have to do with the thought pattern of each of the main characters. These messages could also be something which contradicts their reasoning.

The little black record is the "Beautiful Clothes (Nick Rhodes/ Glitter Glam Mix – 7" Edit). There is also a picture of Nick and Warren, which people can see inside the cardboard after the record is opened.

Arguably, the most fascinating part of the package is the little booklet which came with the record in one of the sleeves. First, one sees the introduction written by Nick, as he gives a good summary of the story.

On the opposite side are descriptions of all four characters and additional notes, indicating the types of behaviours the scientists studied. The next section includes some Polaroid pictures taken by Nick as they relate to each character.

Finally, the backside includes acknowledgements and additional information about others who collaborated with Nick and Warren on the completion of the album.

Between March 7 and April 5, 2013, Nick exhibited a collection of some original photos that he had taken in London. The exhibition was to coincide with the release of *Bored with Prozac and The Internet?* The collection included twenty Polaroids and more than thirty other pieces of his original work.

The premier of "Bei Incubi," translated in English as "Beautiful Nightmares," launched at The Vinyl Factory in Chelsea, London on March 7. The next day (through to April 5) the venue was open to the public. Nick explained that the photographs were all taken of the same girl, but she kept on changing throughout the course of the show.

This is very much how celebrities alter their style or appearance to meet the demands of their fans. A lot of the work seems to focus on the daughter, as it is her main obsession to become famous. The whole idea behind the title, "Bei Incubi," is that no matter how perfect something looks on the surface, there is always some kind of visible flaw.

Bored with Prozac and the Internet? was not the only thing Warren Cuccucullo had been working on in the nineties. His 2014 solo album, *The Master*, was a collaboration effort with Ustad Sultan Khan.

Warren became fascinated with Eastern music after his first exposure from watching the *Ed Sullivan Show*, witnessing a performance by Ravi Shankar. He was introduced to Eastern music, at first, via George Harrison. *The Master* came about in 1998, when Ustad and Warren held a recording session. The music was recorded on a 24-track tape. The project was forgotten about until Warren found them and restored the tracks, adding bass and drum tracks, in early 2014.

Although Khan passed away in 2011, Warren has helped keep his legacy alive. *The Master*, which is a blend of Eastern and Western-style music, was released on July 22, 2014. For those who are looking for more information about him and his career, Warren's official website details can be found at the end of the book.

Band Aid 30 also did a remake of the song in 2014 to help promote awareness about the Ebola crisis; all proceeds went toward battling the terrible illness. Some of the lyrics were changed to reflect the current situation. Although Bob Geldof was just as instrumental in this remake, Duran Duran was in no way involved the second time around.

Some of the big names that were involved included One Direction, Sam Smith, Ed Sheeran and Bono (who was involved in all three

Band Aid song recordings). The song was also included in French and German with respective artists.

Ever since early 2014, there had been rumours of Duran Duran releasing a new album. Although the band stayed active and toured a lot during that year, all the major hype concerning the new album had yet to happen.

They started their new album promotional tour on February 15, 2015 at Wilton's Musical Hall in London, England. They continued playing shows in England before heading over to perform some dates in the U.S. The band then closed the tour on December 15, 2015 at Echo Arena in Liverpool.

The long-anticipated single, "Pressure Off" was released in the states on June 19, 2015. The dance track song also featured Janelle Monáe and Nile Rodgers. The lyrics explain the importance of escaping the monotony of everyday life and the work world. While "Pressure Off" received mixed reactions at first, it soon became one of Duran Duran's danceable hits.

John Taylor started off by saying that Mark Ronson suggested that they get together with Nile Rodgers. Needless to say, the band was more than eager to get started. Nick had some input of his own by saying that he enjoyed having them in the same room as each other, especially since that was the first time the two legendary producers had worked together.

Rodgers also had many nice things to say about Duran Duran. Not only had he already done tremendous work with them for *Notorious* but with *Paper Gods*, he further complimented them by saying that Duran Duran was like his second band. Of course, Duran Duran reciprocated by further complimenting Nile's talent.

On June 22, 2015, yet another updated version of *Rio* was released. (The album was previously re-released in July 2001, containing all the songs and an enhanced web link and video section.) The double disc album contains five parts: the original UK album, bonus tracks, the Manchester Square demos, non-album singles and B-sides, and versions and mixes.

Even during their first listen, many fans could most likely tell that the tracks have been remastered, which prominently stands out on tracks such as "Hold Back the Rain" and "New Religion."

The bonus tracks include different remixes of the following songs; "Rio," "My Own Way," "Lonely in Your Nightmare," "Hungry Like the Wolf," and "Hold Back the Rain." The B-side, "Like an Angel" is included in the form of a Manchester Square demo and a non-album B-side. There is also a brief Christmas message from Simon, circa 1982.

The booklet inside contains band photos taken around the time of the album's release, song lyrics, track listings, a brief description of the album, and a piece written by Daryl Easlea. In his essay, Daryl describes the making of *Rio*, everything from Patrick Nagel's creation to where the album was recorded. Some of Daryl's other books include *Without Frontiers: The Life & Music of Peter Gabriel*, *Sparks: Talent Is an Asset*, and *Crazy in Love: The Beyoncé Knowles Biography*.

Their second single from *Paper Gods*, the title track, starts off sounding like a Gregorian chant, segueing into lyrics and music. Once the song gets into full swing, it has an element of sound which is familiar, but it doesn't sound like something which someone would easily associate with Duran Duran.

"You Kill Me with Silence" is the third single off *Paper Gods*. The music and lyrics sound like something off *Red Carpet Massacre*, but the lyrics might also remind one of "Love Voodoo", a song about control and emasculation.

The songs released before the album include "Pressure Off," "Paper Gods," "You Kill Me with Silence," "What Are the Chances?" and "Last Night in the City." The first of the bunch was the featured song from *Paper Gods*.

During the summer of 2015, they were featured many times in various articles and magazines. *Billboard* had paid the band special attention, as their pictures had been splashed all over the magazine.

Five cover photos of the band had been released on June 17, 2015. The results of the shoot included four black and white photos, one for each member of the band. The group colour photo was used for *Billboard*'s July 25, 2015 feature story. The captions under each photo talk about various things, from Simon wanting to be recognised as a "cool" band to Nick being compared to Andy Warhol yet again.

Their July 25 *Billboard* cover story talked about many interesting facts including how they had not even signed with Warner Brothers until the album was nearly completed.

In the short video which accompanied the story, Nick stated that title *Paper Gods* means whatever what fans thought it to mean, it is open to interpretation. Simon said that he was very pleased with the collaborative effort, which eventually saw the album's completion after nearly two years.

Their fourteenth studio album, *Paper Gods*, was released worldwide on September 11, 2015. Around the time of the album's release, "Pressure Off" had climbed the charts to No.38. The album was produced by Nile Rodgers and Mark Ronson. On the date of the album's release, Duran Duran performed at Bestival, Robin Hill Park, Isle of Wight.

Paper Gods contains twelve regular tracks. The Deluxe Edition includes three additional songs, "Planet Roaring," "Valentine Stones," and "Northern Lights." A special edition was also made and sold exclusively at Target stores. The album background colour is pink, as opposed to the blue and pink mixture on the original. The two bonus tracks for this special edition include "On Evil Beach" and "Cinderella Ride."

Lindsey Lohan had sent Nick a text, asking if she could be included on the new album. She was delighted when he responded in the positive, but she showed up two weeks late. Still, Simon and Nick defended her, stating that her work was "brilliant."

Paper Gods had done better than expected. The album debuted at No.10 on the billboard charts, a feat which Duran Duran had not achieved since the release of *The Wedding Album*. As of September 20, 2015, the album had sold 25,000 units. *Paper Gods* is Duran Duran's 6th Top 10 album, following on from *Rio*, *Seven and the Ragged Tiger*, *Duran Duran* (1983 re-release) *Arena*, and *The Wedding Album*.

The album cover was designed by Alex Israel and contains iconic pictures representing their past albums and songs, like the cherry lips from "Rio" and the sumo wrestler from "Girls on Film." In a way, the artwork served as a throwback to their material from the eighties.

Additional musicians include Mr Hudson, Kieska, Janelle Monáe, Nile Rodgers, Jonas Bjerre, John Frusciante, Davide Rossi, and Lindsey Lohan.

The Fresh Fall Fest Concert took place at Madison Square Garden on October 8, 2015. Others who performed included Rachel Platten and Adam Lambert. Duran Duran received top billing. The event was highly publicised and was advertised on various social media sites, such as Twitter and Pinterest.

While Rachel Platten is under Columbia Records, Duran Duran and Adam Lambert both share the Warner Brothers label.

Adam Lambert has achieved massive fame since his 2009 debut on *American Idol*. Despite the fact that Adam was a runner up, having come in second to Kris Allen, his music is much more celebrated and well-known. Adam has since released four solo albums, *For Your Entertainment* (2009), *Trespassing* (2012), *The Original High* (2015), and *Velvet* (2020).

Adam's was also busy travelling around the world and performing with Queen as their lead vocalist. Although Adam is not an official member of Queen, he is very close to the members of the band, especially guitarist Brian May. Reportedly, Adam is also a fan of Duran Duran, and he has also worked with Nile Rodgers.

The long-awaited video for "Pressure Off" was released on October 21, 2015. Just like the one for "All You Need Is Now," this was filmed in black and white. Not only were the four main band members moving around the screen, but the video also featured Nile Rodgers and Janelle Monae.

"Pressure Off" starts with a close-up of Nile playing his guitar. Then, there are shots of each band member. In addition, the video also features dancers busting some fancy moves. The musicians and dancers jumping into the air could be symbolic of literally letting the pressure off their feet, jumping into something new. It was also a nice touch how all the musicians took a bow at the end. Of course, one can view the video on YouTube.

On December 8, 2015, dates were announced for the *Paper Gods Tour*. The first US date of the tour was March 28, 2016 at Durham, NC. It ended on August 3, 2016 in Glendale, Arizona. Special guests included Chic and Nile Rodgers.

It seemed that Andy Taylor had not completely washed his hands of Duran Duran. In February 2016, it was announced that another version of "Save a Prayer" was going to be released. While the song was the same, it seemed to have a completely different sound. Some could describe it as being more synth pop than anything else.

"Save a Prayer (B4L4m Edit)" was a cover version of the original, featuring Thomas Gandy and Andy Taylor. It was said the song was a response to the Paris terrorist attacks which took place on November 13, 2015.

Duran Duran was in Paris during that time. They were part of the 24 Hours of Reality and Live Earth: The World Is Watching global event. The program sought to educate people about the serious issue of climate change. They performed "What Are the Chances?" at 6:00.

The tragic attack took the lives of over 100 people, and Duran Duran didn't hesitate to show their support and sympathy. The remake of "Save a Prayer" seemed to be a touching and appropriate tribute to those who had so recently lost their lives due to such a senseless act of violence.

The *Paper Gods* Tour was well-received, and fans all over the world were happy at the chance to see their favourite band back in action. Nile Rodgers and Chic added extra excitement to what concertgoers had already deemed to be great shows.

****

Duran Duran has done their fair share of covers, expanding beyond the tracks they included on *Thank You*. In return, some other artists have covered their songs as well. In 2017, a seventeen-year-old contestant on *The Voice* sang a beautiful rendition of "Ordinary World" that earned her a standing ovation. "Ordinary World" is a powerful enough song in itself, but when a younger person sings it with such sincerity, they inspire other people their own age to dig back into the music archives and discover some of the classics there. And because of that one performance, Duran Duran's "Ordinary World" rose to popularity on the charts again.

Ernest Cline is the author of the extremely popular *Ready Player One* book series. The first book was released in 2011, and the sequel, *Ready Player Two* came out in 2020. *Ready Player One* was also a wildly successful movie which came out in 2018, and in it are a few pop culture references to Duran Duran. One is when Wade Watts' avatar, briefly dons a "Nick Rhodes Duran Duran" outfit when he is getting ready for his first date with Samantha Cook, aka, Art3mis. The author also makes a reference to the song "Union of the Snake" in the book.

Simon and Yasmin's world changed once again when they became grandparents, or "glamparents" in 2018. The couple's middle child, Saffron, gave birth to their first grandchild Taro Arturo. Just like many other couples, Simon and Yasmin are simply enamoured with their grandson, as they describe his arrival being the catalyst of starting the happiest period of their life.

The family is very close, both figuratively and literally, as Saffron,

Benjamin Compton (her partner) and Taro live in a cottage at the end of Simon and Yasmin's garden. Although Aunt Amber Rose had spread her wings and moved out on her own, Aunt Tallulah is not far away, as she still lives with Simon and Yasmin, as well.

On July 16, 2019, they performed at the Kennedy Space Center Visitor Complex. The occasion was to mark the 50th anniversary of the Apollo 11's successful moon landing. Given some of their sci-fi inspired music, like "Astronaut," the band is fascinated with anything to do with outer space. And in the words of Neil Armstrong, man setting foot on the moon was, indeed, "one giant leap for mankind."

During September 2019, Saffron gave birth to another son, Skye Nouri Compston Le Bon, making Simon and Yasmin grandparents again.

Funko is a toy company that makes large-headed, small-bodies figures for all ages. While there was some talk about possible production of Duran Duran action figures during the early 2000s, Funko made an announcement in late 2019 that they would manufacture and distribute toys based on the popular five-man line-up. Eager fans everywhere were delighted when they finally got their hands on miniature versions of Simon, Nick, John, Andy, and Roger, some of them adding to their already extensive collections.

CHAPTER 15

What Happens Tomorrow?

One never really knows just what's around the corner, as the world can drastically change without any notice. During late 2019 and early 2020, the world had succumbed to the devastating effects of COVID-19, also known as the coronavirus. Performances were cancelled, thus leading to drastic losses of income for performers and their crews. The band had to postpone all their upcoming tour to celebrate their milestone fortieth anniversary as a band. Absolutely no one is immune, as evidence by the fact that John Taylor came down with a mild case. However, it did not take him long to recover, and he maintained a positive attitude during quarantine.

Much of mankind has been negatively affected by the coronavirus, which had led many to reach out and help their fellow man. And Duran Duran are no exception. Along with their friend David Lynch, they have collaborated again to assist medical professionals who are battling and combatting the deadly pandemic.

During the spring of 2020, the partners teamed up with the Health and Wellness of the David Lynch Foundation to initiate a program called Heal Healers Now. The approach is simple. Instead of relying on Western medicine, health care workers are encouraged to use transcendental meditation to ease their stress and anxiety brought upon treating patients who have the virus. The fund receives donations and uses them to provide healthcare workers access to transcendental meditation sessions at no additional charge. The Heal Healers Now Fund is a great way to give back to the most essential workers who fight on the front line every day in order to restore the health of the rest of us.

Their new single, a cover of David Bowie's "Five Years" was released in early 2021 to go hand-in-hand with the musician's tribute for the Save the Children charity. The song's title was pertinent given that David Bowie had passed away five years earlier on January 10, 2016. It also captures the sadness many of us are feeling as we wearily trudge through this troubled world.

The video premiered on YouTube on January 28, 2021. (Yes, I watched it premiere live.) Despite the bleak tone of the song being covered and re-released during COVID-19, the band's beautiful performance is captured with backup singers and musicians in a background full of swirling lights which invoke wonder in the minds of its viewers.

The song was the band's first release since 2015's *Paper Gods*. Not only was the song released as a tribute to David Bowie but to whet the appetites of fans who have been waiting nearly six years for the next album. The album *Future Past* is being co-produced by Erol Aklin and Graham Coxon, guitarist for the band Blur.

The virtual David Bowie tribute, titled "Just for One Day," was streamed live worldwide on January 8, 2021, on what would have been the musician's 74th birthday. Aside from Duran Duran, some of the line-up included well-known entertainers such as Adam Lambert, Boy George, Ricky Gervais and Peter Frampton, as well as many others. The event was very well-received as it was a fitting tribute to one of glam rock's most influential icons.

That wasn't the first time the band paid tribute to David Bowie. They previously covered one of Bowie's hit songs, "Fame," which he wrote with John Lennon and Carlos Alomar. Then again in 2010, they covered a version of "Boys Keep Swinging" a song which Bowie wrote with Brian Eno. The tribute album, *We Are so Turned On* was released via Mamimal Vinyl, and all proceeds from the charity album benefited War Child UK, which is an organisation that gives to children who are negatively impacted by war.

Just like many other performers, they are making plans for 2021 tour dates, including their postponed 2020 concert at Hyde Park.

On January 21, 2021, Nick became the recipient of another award. The Roland Lifetime Achievement Award is given to those who are noted as making great contributions in the music industry while using their brand-name instruments. Nick had received congratulations from some of his peers, who were impressed with his forty plus career so far. Needless to say, Nick was very pleased with his accomplishment.

Not only has Duran Duran been a large part of my life since the year 2000, but they have also given me the hope and inspiration to fulfil my dreams. Their talent enabled them to establish a large fan base and achieve worldwide fame.

One has to remember that they started out releasing their albums on record long before the days of the Internet. Now, they have countless videos on YouTube, including all their *Behind the Music* stories, and their music can be downloaded through iTunes. Through over 100 million record sales in over thirty-five years, they proved their endurance and longevity to their most loyal fans and the world at large.

Duran Duran's name and music will live on for generations to come. With regard to the label "modern classic," they truly deserve all the acclaim they receive. Of course, as these words are read, Duran Duran is making further progress. They are caught up in the excitement that follows them to the studio. The band's great success over nearly forty years proves that they certainly live up to their name, a name which carries a strong meaning. Durability has seen them through, as many loyal fans continue to support their work.

As many have admired their work for years, we find our admiration for the band will continue to grow because of the impact of their music. Duran Duran has made an indelible mark on the world of music, and it shall continue to expand with their career. After all, the English translation of the word and name Duran is, *they last*. This is just another example of Duran Duran's lasting legacy. Many fans from all around the world, will be anxious to find out what happens tomorrow.

Just like life in general, we are not sure what the future holds, but there is always a feeling of hope, which lets everyone believe that everything is going to be all right in the end.

AFTERWORD

Shortly after I finished writing most of my book, I was informed that another unauthorised biography about the band was going to be released. I was also told about some of the extra features the book was going to include, such as interviews from band members and those who were close to them. I was dismayed when I found out about the release of the other biography, but I soon came to realise that I shouldn't have been.

I came very close to scrapping the entire project, but I was informed by my friends and family that I would regret such a hasty decision. So, in essence, I owe the completion of this project to their undying love and support. During the last, few years, I began to rediscover my love for Duran Duran, and I also began to redefine what their music has meant to me over the years.

As I have stated before, Duran Duran is an important part of my life, and they have been one of my greatest inspirations. I also hope many of you out there share some of my viewpoints as I express my adoration for the band which has helped me discover so much through their music.

2021 also marks the fifteenth anniversary of the completion of *Reach up for the Sunrise*. The first edition was released in July of 2006. This new edition includes more current and up-to-date information concerning Duran Duran over the last fifteen years. I did this especially for all the fans who would like to read more.

Duran Duran has done more than withstood the test of time; they have also become a great legend in the making!

For most fans, it's good to know that Duran Duran is getting a chance to enjoy their success all over again. Although some may have expressed their disappointment over the years with the band's changing line-ups, most fans are happy that Duran Duran has regrouped. To some, this constitutes an era. To me, this constitutes a great part of my life. This is why I find myself extremely proud of the band's progress as they have, indeed, lasted a lifetime.

DISCOGRAPHY

Albums

Duran Duran **(1981)**
Girls on Film / Planet Earth / Anyone Out There / To the Shore / Is There Something I Should Know?* / Careless Memories / Night Boat / Sound of Thunder / Friends of Mine / Tel Aviv //
*Not on the original but included on the 1983 reissue.

Rio **(1982)**
Rio / My Own Way / Lonely in Your Nightmare / Hungry Like the Wolf / Hold Back the Rain / New Religion / Last Chance on the Stairway / Save a Prayer / The Chauffeur //

Seven and the Ragged Tiger **(1983)**
The Reflex / New Moon on Monday / (I'm Looking for) Cracks in the Pavement / I Take the Dice / Of Crime and Passion / Union of the Snake / Shadows on Your Side / Tiger Tiger / The Seventh Stranger //

Arena **(Live) (1984)**
Is There Something I Should Know? / Hungry Like the Wolf / New Religion / Save a Prayer / The Wild Boys / The Seventh Stranger / The Chauffeur / Union of the Snake / Planet Earth / Careless Memories //

Notorious **(1986)**
Notorious / American Science / Skin Trade / A Matter of Feeling / Hold Me (demo version "Rope") / Vertigo (Do the Demolition) (demo version "Vertigo") / So Mislead / Meet El Presidente (demo version "One of the Faithful") / Winter Marches On / Proposition //

Big Thing **(1988)**
Big Thing / I Don't Want Your Love / All She Wants Is / Too Late Marlene / Drug (It's Just a State of Mind) / Do You Believe in Shame? / Palomino / Interlude One / Land / Flute Interlude / The Edge of America / Lake Shore Driving //

Liberty **(1990)**
Violence of Summer (Love's Taking Over) / Liberty / Hothead / Serious (demo version "So Serious") / All Along the Water / My Antarctica (demo version "Throb") / First Impression" (demo version "I Don't Want to Turn My Back on You") / Read My Lips" (demo version "Second Alibi") / Can You Deal with It? / Venice Drowning / Downtown / Yo Bad Azizi (bonus track) (demo version "Nuclear War") //

Duran Duran (The Wedding Album) **(1993)**
Too Much Information (demo version "Fireflag") / Ordinary World / Love Voodoo / Drowning Man / Shotgun / Come Undone / Breath After Breath / UMF / None of the Above / Femme Fatale / Shelter (demo version "Shelter of My Heart") / To Whom It May Concern (demo versions "Mr. Jones" and "People") / Sin of the City / Falling Angel (bonus track, aka "Happy Birthday" demo) / Stop Dead (bonus track) / Time for Temptation (bonus track) //

Thank You **(1995)**
White Lines / I Wanna Take You Higher / Perfect Day / Watching the Detectives / Lay Lady Lay / 911 Is a Joke / Success / Crystal Ship / Ball of Confusion / Thank You / Drive By / I Wanna Take You Higher Again / Diamond Dogs / (bonus track) //

Medazzaland **(1997)**
Medazzaland / Big Bang Generation / Electric Barbarella / Out of My Mind (demo version "Before I Die") / Who Do You Think You Are? / Silva Halo / Be My Icon / Buried in the Sand / Michael You've Got a Lot to Answer For / Midnight Sun / So Long Suicide (demo version "Can Can") / Undergoing Treatment / Ball and Chain (bonus track) //

Pop Trash **(2000)**
Someone Else Not Me / Lava Lamp / Playing with Uranium / Hallucinating Elvis / Starting to Remember / Pop Trash Movie / Fragment / Mars Meets Venus / Lady Xanax / The Sun Doesn't Shine Forever / Kiss Goodbye / Last Day on Earth / Prototypes (bonus track) / Alguien Más Que No Soy Yo ("Someone Else Not Me [En Español]" ("Un Autre Que Moi ([En Française]" on the Canadian version) //

Astronaut **(2004)**
(Reach Up for the) Sunrise / Want You More / What Happens Tomorrow / Astronaut / Bedroom Toys / Nice / Taste the Summer / Finest Hour / Chains / One of Those Days / Point of No Return / Still Breathing / Virus (bonus track) //

Red Carpet Massacre **(2007)**
The Valley / Red Carpet Massacre / Nite-Runner / Falling Down / Box Full O' Honey / Skin Divers / Tempted / Tricked Out / Zoom In / She's Too Much / Dirty Great Monster / Last Man Standing / Cry Baby Cry (Japanese version album bonus track) //

All You Need Is Now **(2010)**
All You Need Is Now / Blame the Machines / Being Followed Leave a Light On / Safe (in the Heat of the Moment) / Girl Panic! / A Diamond in the Mind / The Man Who Stole a Leopard / Other People's Lives / Mediterranea / Too Bad You're so Beautiful Runway Runaway / Return to Now / Before the Rain / Networker Nation / (bonus track on album CD/DVD combo) / All You Need Is Now / (F.Y.E. exclusive remix) / Early Summer Nerves" (bonus track on certain versions) / This Lost Weekend (on Limited Vinyl Collector's Edition) / Too Close to the Sun (Best Buy International Deluxe CD) //

Paper Gods **(2015)**
Paper Gods / Last Night in the City / You Kill Me with Silence / Pressure Off / Face for Today / Danceophobia / What Are the Chances? / Sunset Garage / Change the Skyline / Butterfly Girl / Only in Dreams / The Universe Alone / Planet Roaring" (bonus track for the Deluxe Edition) / Valentine Stones (bonus track for the Deluxe Edition) / Northern Lights (bonus track for the Deluxe Edition) / On Evil Beach (Target Exclusive Edition) / Cinderella Ride (Target Exclusive Edition) / As Seen from a Distance (limited-edition white *Paper Gods* box set) //

Miscellaneous/B-Sides

"Reincarnation" (1979 demo)
"See Me, Repeat Me" (1979 demo)
"Working the Steel" (1979 demo)
"Tel Aviv" (original version)
"Khanada" ("Careless Memories" B-side)
"Like an Angel" ("My Own Way" B-side)
"Fame" ("Planet Earth" B-side)
"Late Bar" (Planet Earth" B-side)
"Faith in This Colour" ("Is There Something I Should Know?" B-side)
"Secret Oktober" ("Union of the Snake" B-side)
"Seven and the Ragged Tiger" (*Seven and the Ragged Tiger* demo)
"A View to a Kill (That Fatal Kiss)" ("A View to a Kill B-side")
"Anything for You" (*Notorious* demo)
"Berlin" (*Notorious* demo)
"Capitol Chill" (*Notorious* demo)
"One of the Faithful" (*Notorious* demo)
"Take It to Me" (*Notorious* demo)
"We Need You" ("Skin Trade" B-side)
"Bomb" (*Big Thing* demo)
"Do You Believe in Faith" (*Big Thing* demo)
"I am the Medicine" (*Big Thing* demo)
"Pressure" (*Big Thing* demo)
"Sex" (*Big Thing* demo)
"Voodoo Echo" (*Big Thing* demo)
"God (London)" ("Do You Believe in Shame?" B-side)
"This Is How a Road Gets Made" ("Do You Believe in Shame?" B-side)
"Bottleneck" (*Liberty* demo)
"Dream Nation" (*Liberty* demo)
"Firefly" (*Liberty* demo)
"I Won't Turn My Back for You" (*Liberty* demo)

"In Between Woman" (*Liberty* demo)
"Hymn for the Preacher" (*Liberty* demo)
"Juice" (*Liberty* demo)
"Money on Your Side" (*Liberty* demo)
"My Family" (*Liberty* demo)
"Stop the Violence" (*Liberty* demo)
"Water Babies" (*Liberty* demo)
"Worth Waiting For" (*Liberty* demo)
"Do You Wanna Turn Me On?" (*The Wedding Album* demo)
"Matter of Fact" (*The Wedding Album* demo)
"Needle and the Damage Done" ("Perfect Day B-side")
"Jeepster" (*Thank You* demo)
"Butt Naked" (*Medazzaland* demo)
"P.L. You" (*Medazzaland* demo)
"Plastic Girl" (*Medazzaland* demo)
"Swimming with Sharks" (*Medazzaland* demo)
"Sinner or Saint" ([demo version "Trippy Time"] "Out of My Mind" B-side)
"Burning the Ground" (*Greatest*)
"Decadance" (B-side to "Burning the Ground")
"Beautiful Colours" (*Astronaut* demo)
"Lonely Business" (*Astronaut* demo)
"Pretty Ones" (*Astronaut* demo)
"Salt in the Rainbow" (*Astronaut* demo)
"TV vs. Radio" (*Astronaut* demo)
"Know It All" ("[Reach up for the Sunrise]" demo)
"Silent Icy River" ("What Happens Tomorrow" B-side)
"Boys Keep Swinging" (2010 David Bowie Tribute, *We Are so Turned On* charity album)
"Make Me Smile ([Come up and See Me]" Cockney Rebel cover – B-side to "The Reflex")
"Five Years" (David Bowie cover for 2021 tribute album)

Compilations

Decade (1989)
Greatest (1998)
Night Versions: The Essential Duran Duran (1998)
Strange Behaviour (1999)
Singles Box Set 1981-1985 (2003)
Singles Box Set 1986-1995 (2004)
Only After Dark (John Taylor and Nick Rhodes) (2006)

*There is a great deal of information that I found extremely helpful through these sources as well as the others listed in the bibliography section.

Videos/DVDs

ExtraOrdinary World (1994)
Sing Blue Silver (2004)
Greatest (2003)
Arena (2004)
Astronaut (2004)
Duran Duran: Live from London (2005)
Red Carpet Massacre (2007)
Duran Duran: Classic Albums: Rio (2008)
Duran Duran Live at Hammersmith '82 (2009)
All You Need Is Now (2010)
A Diamond in the Mind (2012)
Unstaged (2015)

REFERENCES

Official Band Member Websites:
Duran Duran:
duranduranmusic.com
http://duranduran.warnereprise.com/

Warren Cuccurullo:
http://www.warrencuccurullo.com/

Duran Duran Timeline:
https://duranduran.fandom.com/wiki/Duran_Duran_-_Timeline_Index

Additional Sites
Facebook: http://www.facebook.com/duranduran

Instagram: https://www.instagram.com/duranduran/

MySpace: http://www.myspace.com/duranduran

Pinterest: https://www.pinterest.com/PinDuranDuran/

Soundcloud: https://soundcloud.com/duranduran

Spotify:
https://play.spotify.com/artist/0lZoBs4Pzo7R89JM9lxwoT?play=true&utm_source=open.spotify.com&utm_medium=open

Tumblr: https://duranduranofficial.tumblr.com/

Twitter: https://twitter.com/No.!/duranduran

YouTube: https://www.youtube.com/user/07DuranDuran?feature=guide

Rock and Roll Hall of Fame Petition:
http://www.thepetitionsite.com/1/duran-duran-to-the-rock-hall-of-fame/

"Save a Prayer" remake: https://www.youtube.com/watch?v=Rru-oQqkEAg

Other References
Adrianson, Doug. "Duran Duran Tries Harder Rock." Miami Herald. January 13, 1989.

"All Rhodes Lead to Nick." UK Daily Mail. 02/21/02.

Alphabetical Survey of Requiem Composers.
http://www.requiemsurvey.org/

"American Express Launches Second Year of 'Unstaged' Music Series with Iconic Pairing: Duran Duran and Filmaker David Lynch. (NY-AmEx-Duran-Duran.)" PR Newswire. March 14, 2011.

Aniftos, Rania. "Check out the Full Star-Studded Line-up for Virtual David Bowie Tribute "Just for One Day." Billboard. January 6, 2021.
https://www.billboard.com/articles/columns/rock/9474032/a-bowie-celebration-just-for-one-day-line-up/

Aquilante, Dan. "Duran Duran Fans Get a Double Dose." New York Post. 1997.

"A View to a Spill. (Drowning Experience.) Simon Le Bon." People Weekly. August 26, 1985.

"Bei Incubi: 'Beautiful Nightmares' to Celebrate the Launch of TV Mania's New Album: 'Bored with Prozac and the Internet?' " London. March 7, 2013. February 26th, 2013.
http://www.duranduran.com/wordpress/2013/bei-incubi-beautiful-nightmares-to-celebrate-the-launch-of-tv-manias-new-album-bored-with-prozac-and-the-internet-london-march-7-2013/

Bored with Prozac and the Internet? TV Mania. Magus Entertainment, 2013.

Bosarge, Charlotte. "He's Just a Regular Joe with a Regular Job." Seattlesquare.com, 1998.

Bowar, Chad. "Entering Medazzaland with Duran Duran." October 24, 1997.

Campbell, Mary. "Duran Duran Sighs with Relief, Breaks into the '90s." Associated Press. April 9, 1993.

DeGraff, Kasper. Garrett, Malcolm. Duran Duran: Their Story.
Proteus Publishing Co. Inc.; New York, 1982.

Dickinson, Chris. "Robert Palmer's Power Station Brings Back the Funk Back to Mississippi Nights." St. Louis Post Dispatch. 1997.

www.dombrown.com Bio:
http://www.dombrown.com/bio.html

Downes, Catherine. "Duran Duran's Roger Taylor Tells Us Why He Wishes He'd Kept His '80s Wardrobe." Dallas Observer. October 4, 2011. http://blogs.dallasobserver.com/dc9/2011/10/post_16.php

Duffy, Thom. "Duran Duran on Track for a '93 World Comeback." Billboard. June 26, 1993.

Duerdon, Nick. "Billboard Cover: Duran Duran on Pushing the Pop Envelope, Staying Power and Why Harry Styles Is a 'Good Chap'." Billboard. July 17, 2015. http://www.billboard.com/articles/columns/rock/6634365/duran-duran-paper-gods-album-interview-legacy-one-direction

Duran Duran. All You Need Is Now. Skin Divers Music Video. Filmed and edited by Gavin Elder. Skin Divers and S-Curve Records, 2011.

Duran Duran. "All You Need Is Now." S-Curve Records, 2011. Uploaded January, 21, 2011 by DuranDuran VEVO.
http://www.youtube.com/watch?v=VvqnJ8AGhFg&ob=av3n

"Duran Duran Announce Four Intimate Rehearsal Shows for UK Fans." PR Newswire Europe. August 24, 2011.
https://www.prnewswire.co.uk/news-releases/duran-duran-announce-four-intimate-rehearsal-shows-for-uk-fans-145090825.html

Duran Duran. Arena. EMI Records Video. Directed by Russell Mulcahy. EMI Records Ltd., 2004.

Duran Duran. Astronaut. Epic Music Video. Directed by Gavin Elder. Epic Records, 2004.

"Duran Duran Baffled, Too, By Tribute Album." Orange County Register. October 3, 1997.

Duran Duran: The Billboard Cover Shoot. Billboard. 7/17/15.
http://www.billboard.com/photos/6633654/duran-duran-billboard-photo-shoot-cover-story/5

Duran Duran. A Diamond in the Mind. Eagle Vision Video. Directed by Gavin Elder. Eagle Rock Entertainment Ltd., 2011.

"Duran Duran Drummer Weds." May 27. 2007.

Duran Duran. Duran Duran: Classic Albums: Rio. Eagle Vision Video. Directed by George Scott. Eagle Rock Entertainment Ltd., 2008.

Duran Duran. ExtraOrdinary World. Picture Music International Video. Directed by Allie Eberhardt. EMI Records, Ltd.,1994.

Duran Duran. "Girl Panic!" Skin Divers Music, 2011. Published November 8, 2011 by DuranDuran VEVO.
http://www.youtube.com/watch?v=sSMbOuNBV0s

Duran Duran. Greatest. EMI Music Video. EMI Records Ltd, 2003.
"Duran Duran's John Taylor Honoured as Musician-Author Accepts Writers in Treatment's Experience, Strength & Hope Award." Duran Duran.com. February 19, 2013.
http://www.duranduran.com/wordpress/2013/duran-durans-john-taylor-honoured-as-musician-author-accepts-writers-in-treatments-experience-strength-hope-award/

Duran Duran Fan Community. "John Taylor's New Book!" May, 2012.
https://www.duranduranmusic.com/?page=news_item&NewsID=3765647605946&Press_Page_Width=750&last_page=news_archive

Duran Duran. Live at Hammersmith '82. Capitol Records Video. Capitol Records. 2009.

Duran Duran. Live from London. CHS/DD LLC Zoë Video. Directed by Lawrence Jordan. CHS/DD LLC Zoë, 2005.

"Duran Duran Makes Grand Reentrance." Billboard. January 30, 1993.

Duran Duran Fan Community. "Duran Duran's Nick Rhodes to Receive Honorary Doctorate."

Duran Duran Fan Community. "Duran Duran to Play at Olympic Opening Ceremonies!" Duran Duran.com. May, 2012.
http://www.duranduranmusic.com/?page=news_item&NewsID=3765647606092&Press_Page_Width=750&last_page=news_archive

Duran Duran: "Pressure Off" (The Making of)
https://www.youtube.com/watch?v=BHFaSv0UzU4

Duran Duran. Red Carpet Massacre. Epic Music Video. Filmed and edited by Gavin Elder. Skin Divers and S-Curve Records, 2007.

Duran Duran – Reportage. December 26, 2009.
http://www.youtube.com/watch?v=FPYRgxgI2DU

Duran Duran Rocked the Rocket Garden at Kennedy Space Center Visitor Complex with Concert and Choreographed Drone Light Performance by Studio Drift By: PR Newswire, PR Newswire US, 07/18/2019.
https://www.prnewswire.com/news-releases/duran-duran-rocked-the-rocket-garden-at-kennedy-space-center-visitor-complex-with-concert-and-choreographed-drone-light-performance-by-studio-drift-300887468.html

Duran Duran "Rolling Stone's Most Anticipated Albums of 2021." January 20, 2021. http://www.duranduran.com/wordpress/2021/duran-duran-rolling-stones-most-anticipated-albums-of-2021/

"Duran Duran to the Rock Hall of Fame." http://www.thepetitionsite.com/1/duran-duran-to-the-rock-hall-of-fame/

Duran Duran – Song List
https://duranduran.fandom.com/wiki/Duran_Duran_-_Song_List

Duran Duran. Sing Blue Silver. EMI Music Video. Directed by Michael Collins. EMI Records Ltd.

Duran Duran Wiki We Are so Turned on: A Tribute to David Bowie.
https://duranduran.fandom.com/wiki/We_Were_So_Turned_On:_A_Tribute_To_David_Bowie

Duran Duran Talk REPORTAGE. October 16, 2012.
http://www.youtube.com/watch?v=92i65HogPMk

Duran Duran Wiki MTV Unplugged (2015) http://duranduran.wikia.com/wiki/MTV_Unplugged

Easlea, Daryl. (Untitled Essay.) Rio. 2015
"For Duran Duran, That Was Then, This is 'Now.'" USA Today. January 3, 2011.

Glass, Cyndi. "John Taylor Leaves Duran Duran." Privacy: The Warren Cuccurullo Newsletter. Vol. 4 No.2 Winter 1996/97 Issue 20.

Goddard, Kay. Duran Duran: This Is Your Life. 1983.

Goldstein, Toby. Everything You Want to Know About Duran Duran. Ballantine Books; New York, 1984.

Graff, Gary. "It's No Big Thing: Duran Duran Crew Seems Glad to Put Glory Days to Rest." The Arizona Republic. February 1, 1989.

Green, Jo-Anne. "A Fresh Look at a Pop Music Dynasty." Goldmine Magazine. January 16, 1998.

Green, Jo-Anne. "Your Mission Barbarella: Find Duran Duran." 1998.

Hauptfuhrer, Fred. "Wedding Bells Toll for Duran Duran's Nick Rhodes, Who Marries and Iowa Heiress." People Weekly. September 3, 1984.

Hayes, Kelvin. "Steve Ferrone." Yahoo! 2005.

IMDB. http://www.imdb.com/name/nm0822694 (Claire Stansfield)

IMDB. http://www.imdb.com/name/nm0852616/ (John Taylor)

IMDB. http://www.imdb.com/name/nm1285494 (Meredith Ostrom)

Irwin, Colin. "A View to Another Kill." BBC Teletext. June 11, 1998.

Kent, Cynthia. Duran Duran. Kenzington Publishing Corp; New York, 1984.

Kappes, Serena. "Duran Duran at iHeartRadio Music Festival 2015: Lindsay Lohan's Cameo on New Album 'Paper Gods' Was 'Utterly Brilliant.' " 9/19/15
http://www.billboard.com/articles/columns/music-festivals/6700646/duran-duran-iheartradio-music-festival-2015-paper-gods-lindsay-lohan
John Taylor Celebrity Skin. 11/01/00.

Launch Radio Networks. "Chic/Power Station Drummer Tony Thompson Dead." 11/14/03.

"Lock Up the Women, They're Back!" SMUG Magazine. 1997.

LoMonico, Maura. "Pavarotti Makes Questionable Friends in Bosnia Benefit." The Johns Hopkins Newsletter.

Malins, Steve. Notorious. Andre Deutsch; London, 2005.

Means, Andrew. "Duran Redux Fab Three Put Forth New Lucid Tunes with Drama." The Arizona Republic." July 23, 1987.

Means, Andrew. "Missing Pieces: Duran Duran Finally Has Its Act Together." The Arizona Republic. July 21, 1987.

Mizzoguchi, Karen. Leonard, Elizabeth. "David Lynch and Duran Duran Launch Initiative for Medical Professionals Fighting Coronavirus." People. May 4, 2020.
https://people.com/music/david-lynch-duran-duran-medical-professionals-transcendental-meditation-coronavirus/

Monthly DD Blast. March 3, 2012 DDList@DuranDuranMusic.com

Morrison, Tim. "Q&A Duran Duran." Time. January 10, 2011.

MTV Networks. Biography: Warren Cuccurullo. VH1.com

Murphy, Sandra. "Supermodel Yasmin Le Bon Reveals How She's Loving Life as a Glam Granny." Extra.ie. March 16, 2019.
https://extra.ie/2019/03/16/entertainment/celebrity/yasmin-le-bon-reveals-how-shes-loving-her-new-role-as-glam-granny

"Naked Artist Used Her Body to Paint on (and Behind) Canvas in Bizarre Love Performance." Daily Mail Reporter. April 28, 2009. http://www.dailymail.co.uk/tvshowbiz/article-1174285/Naked-artist-used-body-paint-canvas-bizarre-live-performance.html

Parker, Lyndsey. Careless Memories of My Strange Behavior: My Notorious Life as a Duran Duran Fan. Rhino; 2012.

Parker, Lyndsey. "EXCLUSIVE: Introducing Allison Iraheta and Halo Circus!" February 21, 2013.
http://ca.music.yahoo.com/blogs/reality-rocks/exclusive-introducing-allison-iraheta-halo-circus-225458456.html

Patrick O'Hearn.
http://www.united-mutations.com/o/patrick_ohearn.htm

Payne, Chris. July 17, 2015. "Duran Duran, Nile Rodgers & Mark Ronson Team Up to Take the 'Pressure Off': Behind-the-Scenes Video." Billboard. http://www.billboard.com/articles/columns/rock/6634537/duran-duran-nile-rodgers-mark-ronson-pressure-off-video-studio-behind-scenes

Randee, Dawn. "Wild Boys on Broadway. Billboard. 11/17/2007, Vol. 119 Issue 46, p18-18, 1/2p.

Rebaza, Claudia. "Elemental Duran Duran: Songwriting and Style." 1984-1999.

Reesman, Bryan. "Welcome to Medazzaland." Mix Magazine. 1997.

Rhodes, Dean. "Duran Duran, D'Arby Show Comebacks Right on Track." The Phoenix Gazette. August 14, 1993.

Rhodes, Dean. "Video Vs. Music: Duran Duran Climbs Charts with Ballad." The Phoenix. August 13, 1993.

Robinson, Lisa. "Duran Duran Tones It Down." New York Post. 1997.
"Roland Lifetime Achievement Award Presented to Nick Rhodes for His Incredible Contribution to the Music Industry." January 21, 2021.
https://duranduranmusic.com/?page=news_item&NewsID=3765647638679&Press_Page_Width=750&last_page=news_archive

Scaggs, Austin. "Duran Duran Go Back to the Eighties with Mark Ronson." Rolling Stone. 1/20/11 Issue 1122 p. 24-24;2/3p.

Scapelliti, Christopher. "Warren Cuccurullo Releases 'Long-Lost' Album." July 24, 2014.

Sheffield, Rob. Talking to Girls About Duran Duran. Plume; New York, 2010.

Stosuy, Brandon. "Rock Hall 2011 Nominees Announced, Sorry Duran Duran." Stereogum. September 28, 2010.
http://stereogum.com/527361/rock-hall-2011-nominees-announced-sorry-duran-duran/top-stories/

Sullivan, Jim. "Duran Duran the Comeback 'Kids'." The Globe. July 23, 1993.

Taylor, Andy. Wild Boy: My Life in Duran Duran. Grand Central Publishing; New York, 2008.

Taylor, John. In the Pleasure Groove: Love, Death & Duran Duran. New York; Dutton, 2012.

Thapa, Sashi. "All Duran Crowd Needs Is Now." Herald Sun. March 30, 2012.

Thomas Gandey feat. Andy Taylor - Save a Prayer (B4L4m Edit). March 8, 2016.
https://www.youtube.com/watch?v=Rru-oQqkEAg

"Topper Quickly Getting Over Tinsley Mortimer." New York Post. April 27, 2010.
http://www.nypost.com/p/pagesix/topper_fast_getting_over_tins_AvSizeowUjJUYQ5pr5vgAO

Vaziri, Aidin. "Duran Duran Jams at Filmore." San Francisco Chronicle. July 9, 2009.
https://www.sfgate.com/music/article/Music-review-Duran-Duran-jams-at-Fillmore-3292708.php

Wallace, Carol. "A Week Simon Won't Forget-Though He'd Love to." People Weekly. August 26, 1985.

Walters, Barry. "Q&A: Duran Duran's Nick Rhodes on Releasing His Long-Lost Side Project. Keyboardist misplaced 1996 concept album about fame-seeking family." Rolling Stone. March 11, 2013.
http://www.rollingstone.com/music/news/q-a-duran-durans-nick-rhodes-on-releasing-his-long-lost-side-project-20130311

Watson, Ben. Frank Zappa: The Negative Dialectics of Poodle Play. St Martin's Griffin; New York, 1993.

Westbrook, Bruce. "Duran 'Back' with Album, Summer Tour." Houston Chronicle. August 10, 1993.

Widran, Jonathon. "Duran Duran Fighting for Their Liberty." Music Connection.

Wikipedia. Band Aid (1984).
https://en.wikipedia.org/wiki/Band_Aid_(band)

Wikipedia. Reportage (Album) 2013.
https://en.wikipedia.org/wiki/Reportage_(album)
Wikipedia. Robert Palmer
https://en.wikipedia.org/wiki/Robert_Palmer_(singer)No.:~:text=Robert%20Allen%20Palmer%20(19%20January,%2C%20pop%2C%20reggae%20and%20blues.

Wikipedia. "Sterling Campbell." 2005. http://en.wikipedia.org/wiki/Sterling_Campbell

Wooten, Kristi York. "Embracing the Return of Duran Duran's 'Ordinary World.'" Paste Magazine. March 21, 2017.
https://www.pastemagazine.com/music/duran-duran/embracing-the-return-of-duran-durans-ordinary-worl-1/

ABOUT THE AUTHOR

Jen Selinsky was born in Pittsburgh, Pennsylvania. In 2003, she earned her bachelor's degree in English from Clarion University of Pennsylvania. In 2004, she earned her master's degree in library science from the same school. Jen is a semi-retired librarian. She has published more than 200 books, many of which contain poetry. Her work can be found on the following sites: Amazon, Lulu, Barnes & Noble, Kobo, iTunes, Smashwords, Pen It! Publications, and Books-A-Million, as well as many others. She has also been featured in publications such as *The Courier Journal*, *The News and Tribune*, *Pen It!* Magazine, *Explorer* Magazine, *Liphar* Magazine, and *Indiana Libraries*. She works as the Senior Editor for Pen It! Publications and also edits for *Pen It!* Magazine, Hydra Publications, and Write Your Best Book. One of her children's books, *You Are You!* won the IMADJINN Award for Best Children's Book 2019. Jen lives in Sellersburg, Indiana with her husband.